Steck Vaughn

Level D

Vocabulary Connections

Program Consultants

Dr. Barbara Coulter

Director, Department of Communication Arts

Detroit Public Schools

Dr. Catherine C. Hatala

Director, Reading/English Language Arts

School District of Philadelphia

Harcourt Achieve

Rigby · Steck-Vaughn

www.HarcourtAchieve.com

1.800.531.5015

ILLUSTRATIONS

Cover: Ed Lindlof
Content Area Logos: Skip Sorvino

Donna Ayers 56–57, 84–87, 89, 104, 107; Heidi Chang 12–15, 17, 50, 52, 91–92, 94, 105, 108–109, 113; Nancy Didion 7–9, 11; Eldon Doty 31–33, 35; Leslie Dunlap 24–25, 28; Nancy Howard 18–20, 22; Pamela Johnson 36–39, 41, 71–72, 74, 76, 96–98, 100, 115–116, 118, 120–122, 124; Linda Knox 59; Bob Lange 48–49, 67–68, 70; Ann Neumann 43–44; 46; Marcia Sewall 60–63, 65, 80–81, 83.

PHOTOGRAPHY

P. 5 © Larry Lefever/Grant Heilman Photography; p. 6 © Emil Schulthess/Black Star; p. 12 © Bettmann/CORBIS; p. 23 © Odile Noel/Sygma; p. 26 © Laser Spectacles; p. 29 © Larry Lefever/Grant Heilman Photography; p. 30 © USDA Photo, Science Source/Photo Researchers; p. 42 © George Porter, National Audubon Society/Photo Researchers; p. 47 © Biophoto Assoicates/Photo Researchers; p.53 © Archive Photos; p. 54 © Robert Azzi/Woodfin Camp & Associates; p. 55 © Stock Boston; p. 66 © NASA/Black Star; p. 73 © Abbas/Magnum Photos; p. 77 © Art Bilstein, National Audubon Society/Photo Researchers; pp.78–79 © UPI/Bettmann/Corbis; p. 90 © Keith Gunnar/Photo Researchers; p. 95 © Allsport; p. 101 © Topham/The Image Works; pp. 102–103, 105 © Culver Pictures; p. 114 © Movie Still Archives; p. 119 © David Young-Wolff/PhotoEdit.

Additional photography by Photos.com Royalty Free.

ACKNOWLEDGMENTS

Abingdon Press: From *Thomas Alva Edison, Inventor.* Copyright renewal © 1981 by Ruth Cromer Weir Dimond. Used by permission of the publisher, Abingdon Press.

HarperCollins Publishers: Adaptation from Chapter 9 of *Stone Fox* by John Reynolds Gardiner. TEXT COPYRIGHT © 1980 BY JOHN REYNOLDS GARDINER. Used by permission of HarperCollins Publishers.

Highlights for Children, Inc.: "Mountain Mist" by Pam Sandlin from *Highlights for Children*, February 1988. Copyright © 1988 by Highlights for Children, Inc., Columbus, Ohio.

Macmillan Publishing Company: Pronunciation Key, reprinted with permission of the publisher from the *Macmillan School Dictionary 2*. Copyright © 1990 Macmillan Publishing Company, a division of Macmillan, Inc.

Chrysalis Books Group (Pavilion): "The Mango Tree," from *Seasons of Splendour* by Madhur Jaffrey. Copyright © 1985 by Madhur Jaffrey. Reprinted by permission of Chrysalis Books Group (Pavilion).

Gail Provost: From *Popcorn* by Gail and Gary Provost. Copyright © 1985 by Gail and Gary Provost. Reprinted by permission of Gail Provost.

ISBN 0-7398-9171-5

© 2004 Harcourt Achieve Inc.

2 3 4 5 6 7 8 073 11 10 09 08 07 06 05

TABLE OF CONTENTS

CONTENT AREA SYMBOLS · · · · 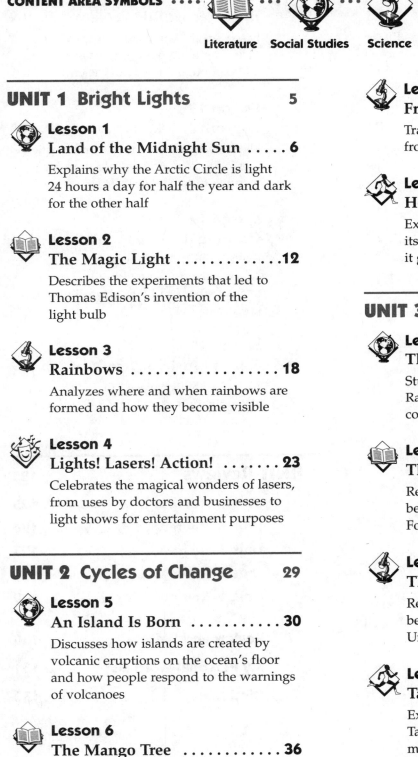 · · ·

Literature   Social Studies   Science   Mathematics   Health   Fine Arts

UNIT 1 Bright Lights   5

Lesson 1
Land of the Midnight Sun **6**
Explains why the Arctic Circle is light
24 hours a day for half the year and dark
for the other half

Lesson 2
The Magic Light **12**
Describes the experiments that led to
Thomas Edison's invention of the
light bulb

Lesson 3
Rainbows **18**
Analyzes where and when rainbows are
formed and how they become visible

Lesson 4
Lights! Lasers! Action! **23**
Celebrates the magical wonders of lasers,
from uses by doctors and businesses to
light shows for entertainment purposes

UNIT 2 Cycles of Change   29

Lesson 5
An Island Is Born **30**
Discusses how islands are created by
volcanic eruptions on the ocean's floor
and how people respond to the warnings
of volcanoes

Lesson 6
The Mango Tree **36**
Shares a legend of how a man and a
mango tree are connected and how a
sister shows her love for both

Lesson 7
From Tadpole to Frog **42**
Traces the stages of a frog's development
from egg to tadpole to frog

Lesson 8
How Does Your Skin Grow? . . **47**
Explains the structure of skin, including
its layers and their functions, and how
it grows

UNIT 3 Wild Races   53

Lesson 9
The King's Camel Race **54**
Studies Saudi Arabia's King's Camel
Race, in which hundreds of riders
compete for prizes

Lesson 10
The Race **60**
Recounts the drama of a dog race
between little Willy and his dog and Stone
Fox and his team of dogs

Lesson 11
The Great Space Race **66**
Relates an account of the Space Race
between the Soviet Union and the
United States

Lesson 12
Tarahumara Racers **71**
Examines a 90-mile race run by the
Tarahumara Indians over the rugged
mountains of northern Mexico

UNIT 4 Mountains' Mysteries 77

Lesson 13
Climbing Mount Everest 78
Chronicles the journey of Edmund Hillary and Tenzing Norgay as they attempt to climb the highest mountain in the world

Lesson 14
Mountain Mist 84
Tells the story of a girl who ignores her mother's warning and ends up lost in the mountain fog

Lesson 15
A Wonder of Nature 90
Describes the formation of the Rocky Mountains, including the snowcapped peaks, dark gorges, and huge caverns

Lesson 16
A "Peak" Experience 95
Explains how Outward Bound teaches young people of varying abilities to become successful mountain climbers

UNIT 5 On Stage 101

Lesson 17
Big Screen, Little Screen 102
Discusses the early years of television, including the types of shows available and a popular comedy of the era

Lesson 18
Popcorn 108
Narrates an aspiring rock star's reaction to a letter from a recording company wanting to review his best songs

Lesson 19
Creating the Impossible 114
Explores the exciting world of special effects, including the techniques used to create them and why the techniques keep changing

Lesson 20
Tejano Music, a New Mix ... 119
Analyzes the popularity of Tejano music, a combination of rock and roll, country, hip-hop, and jazz

UNIT Reviews 125

Unit 1 Review 125
Unit 2 Review 126
Unit 3 Review 127
Unit 4 Review 128
Unit 5 Review 129

Review and Write 130

My Personal Word List 131

Dictionary 133

BRIGHT LIGHTS

The sun lights up the sky in the daytime. The moon and stars give us light at night. Electric light bulbs light up our homes. Our world is filled with light.

In Lessons 1 - 4, you will read about different kinds of light. Think about where light comes from and how it is used. What words come to mind when you think about light? Write your words under the headings below.

Where Light Comes From	How Light Is Used

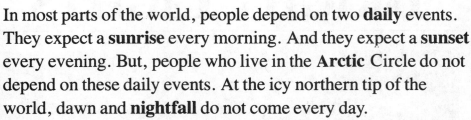

★ Read the story below. Think about the meanings of the **boldfaced** words. ★

Land of the Midnight Sun

In most parts of the world, people depend on two **daily** events. They expect a **sunrise** every morning. And they expect a **sunset** every evening. But, people who live in the **Arctic** Circle do not depend on these daily events. At the icy northern tip of the world, dawn and **nightfall** do not come every day.

The Arctic Circle is near the North Pole. There, from March until September, the sun never drops below the **horizon**. Instead, it stays in the sky all night and all day. It shines with its usual **brightness**. That is why this area is known as "the land of the midnight sun."

This happens because of the **location** of the sun and the earth. The earth travels around the sun once each year. As the earth moves, sunlight hits different parts of it at different angles. The earth also spins. It makes one turn each day. This causes day and night in most parts of the world.

At the North Pole it is different. The earth's spinning does not always make the sun disappear from view. Instead, the sun stays overhead for six months. During that time, it is always daylight!

Not everyone would like to live around the North Pole. People would miss **twilight**. Twilight is the time of day when the sun has set before it gets completely dark. People also would miss seeing **moonlit** nights.

However, the people in "the land of the midnight sun" are not always without moonlight. They have moonlight during the other six months. Then it is dark all day and all night. During these months people spend most of their time indoors. They play games, study, and work to while away the hours of darkness.

★ Go back to the story. Underline the words or sentences that give you a clue to the meaning of each **boldfaced** word. ★

USING CONTEXT

Meanings for the vocabulary words are given below. Go back to the story and read each sentence that has a vocabulary word. If you still cannot tell the meaning, look for clues in the sentences that come before and after the one with the vocabulary word. Write each word in front of its meaning.

brightness	twilight	horizon	location
nightfall	sunset	daily	moonlit
sunrise	Arctic		

1. _____ : the region around the North Pole

2. _____ : the line where the earth and the sky meet

3. _____ : the time when the sun goes down; sundown

4. _____ : the time when the sun comes up in the morning; dawn

5. _____ : the time of day between sundown and complete darkness; dusk

6. _____ : happening every day

7. _____ : the coming of darkness at the end of the day

8. _____ : lighted by the moon

9. _____ : the place where someone or something is located

10. _____ : the quality of being bright

COMPOUND WORDS

A **compound word** is made up of two or more words. For example, <u>sail</u> and <u>boat</u> make up the compound word <u>sailboat</u>. Join one word from Column A with one from Column B to make four compound words. Write the new words.

Column A	Column B
moon	set
night	rise
sun	fall
sun	lit

1. _____

2. _____

3. _____

4. _____

CLOZE PARAGRAPH

Use the words in the box to complete the paragraphs. Reread the paragraphs to be sure they make sense.

Arctic	**location**	**brightness**
daily	**twilight**	**horizon**

Eskimos are people who live in the cold lands of the

(1) _____. The (2) _____ of the Eskimos' land is very far north. So for part of the year, the sun's

(3) _____ lights the sky. Then

(4) _____ activities like fishing and hunting can be done all day and all night.

Later the sun sinks below the (5) _____.

The Eskimos watch the (6) _____ begin. They know darkness and winter will follow.

8

WORD PUZZLE

Write a word from the box next to each clue. Then read the words formed by the letters in the squares. You will have the answer to this riddle.

Why did the mother enjoy waking her son?

She liked to see _____ _____ _____!

daily	brightness	Arctic	nightfall
horizon	sunset	twilight	moonlit
sunrise	locations		

comenos intenso

1. dim light before dark

2. when darkness comes

3. quality of being bright

4. also called sundown

5. lighted by the moon

6. line where the earth and sky meet

7. very cold region that is home to Eskimos and reindeer

8. happening every day

9. positions

10. happening in the morning

9

GET WISE TO TESTS

Directions: Fill in the space for the word that fits best in the sentence.

 Be sure to mark the answer space correctly. Do <u>not</u> mark the circle with an X or with a checkmark (✓). Instead, fill in the circle neatly and completely with your pencil.

1. I eat an apple every day. It is my _____ treat.
   Ⓐ vegetable   Ⓒ daily
   Ⓑ Saturday   Ⓓ arctic

2. It was between sundown and complete darkness. It was _____.
   Ⓕ black   Ⓗ sunrise
   Ⓖ twilight   Ⓙ morning

3. The day begins at dawn. Dawn is also called _____.
   Ⓐ sunrise   Ⓒ night
   Ⓑ sunset   Ⓓ afternoon

4. The sky is full of color as the sun goes down. It is _____.
   Ⓕ sunrise   Ⓗ morning
   Ⓖ sunset   Ⓙ noon

5. Reindeer live around the North Pole. They live in the _____.
   Ⓐ jungle   Ⓒ Arctic
   Ⓑ twilight   Ⓓ river

6. The night sky is bright. It is a _____ sky.
   Ⓕ dark   Ⓗ distant
   Ⓖ sunrise   Ⓙ moonlit

7. It is dark after sundown. _____ follows sundown.
   Ⓐ Afternoon   Ⓒ Nightfall
   Ⓑ Morning   Ⓓ Sunrise

8. The sky seems to meet the land. They meet at the _____.
   Ⓕ horizon   Ⓗ ocean
   Ⓖ station   Ⓙ twilight

9. The sun hurts my eyes today. Its _____ is blinding.
   Ⓐ darkness   Ⓒ distance
   Ⓑ size   Ⓓ brightness

10. We do not know where the store is. We forgot its _____.
    Ⓕ owner   Ⓗ brightness
    Ⓖ location   Ⓙ business

 *Writing*

Imagine that you and your family took a summer trip to "the land of the midnight sun." Write a postcard to a friend. Tell about the sights you have seen. Use the postcard pictures on this page and the pictures in this lesson for ideas. Include some of the facts you have learned in the lesson.

On the lines below, write your postcard. Use some vocabulary words in your writing.

_____
(Date)

Dear _____,

_____

_____

_____

_____

_____

_____

_____

_____

_____

_____

_____

Turn to "My Word List" on page 131. Write some words from the story or other words that you would like to know more about. Use a dictionary to find the meanings.

Your friend,

_____

11

★ Read the story below. Think about the meanings of the **boldfaced** words. ★

The Magic Light

Thomas Alva Edison's life was filled with discovery and disappointment. His many inventions brought sound to our ears and light to our eyes. This is part of his story.

Thomas Edison was determined to make an electric light that would glow with heat. "I must make it **cheaply** enough for everybody to use," he said.

Edison had started one of the greatest inventions of all time. He hired a glass blower to make bulbs. He bought pumps to pump air out of the bulbs. And he thought of new ways to control electric current. He tried many materials to burn inside the bulbs. Sometimes he wondered if anything in the whole world could stand the **intense** heat necessary to **furnish** light.

For more than a year Edison worked on his light. Then one day he called in Charles Batchelor, one of his best scientists.

"Bring in the others who have worked on the light," he said.

The men crowded around as Edison turned on a switch and a bulb lighted. It gave off a bright white light.

"What's wrong with this?" asked one of the men.

"This light is not practical," answered Edison. "In the first place, it would cost too much. It took thirty feet of fine **platinum** wire rolled on a spool."

"Now watch while I turn the electricity a little stronger."

Pfft! Before their eyes, the light burned out. In less than a second the bulb had turned black. The stronger **current** had melted the platinum inside.

Edison went on to explain that in using platinum he had made an important discovery. "When the electricity is turned on, still more air can be pumped from the bulbs. While a bulb burns, we will pump it again. Then we will seal it tightly."

The men started to leave. Each felt new hope and confidence and pride. Each showed a new excitement.

"Wait, Batchelor," Edison said.

Just then an office boy rushed in. "Mrs. Edison said she couldn't imagine what you wanted with ordinary cotton sewing thread," he said. "But she gave it to me. Are you going to use thread in your new light?"

"Perhaps," smiled the **inventor**, reaching for the thread.

Quickly he cut off several small pieces. He bent each piece into a tiny loop shaped like a **horseshoe**.

"Carbonize these pieces of thread," Edison said to Batchelor. To carbonize them, the threads were baked in a hot oven until they were burned black.

"But I thought you had given up **carbon** for light." Batchelor was plainly surprised.

"I am going back to carbon," said Edison. "We can now pump more air from the bulbs. Carbon is still the best material I have found.

"Bring the thread to me as soon as it is done. I will be waiting. And have more bulbs made," Edison added.

Several hours later Batchelor brought the threads. Quickly Edison attached one in a glass bulb.

When the air was pumped out, the bulb was sealed. It was ready for the test. Edison turned on the electricity.

The bulb burned for forty hours. Even while it burned, the inventor was thinking of ways to improve it.

"Carbonized paper should work better than thread," he reasoned. He rolled paper into a thin little roll as fine as thread and sent it to be baked into carbon.

He was right. The paper carbon burned **indefinitely**! People began to read and hear the news of the wonderful light. "Edison is a **wizard**," they declared. "Now he has invented a magic light."

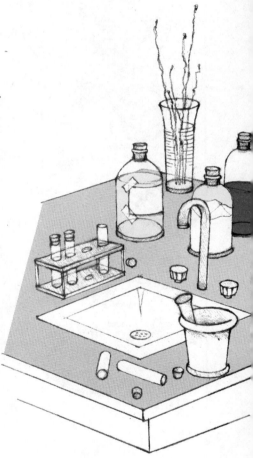

From **Thomas Alva Edison: Inventor**, by Ruth Cromer Weir

★ Go back to the story. Underline any words or sentences that give you clues to the meanings of the **boldfaced** words. ★

CONTEXT CLUES

Read each sentence. Look for clues to help you complete each sentence with a word from the box. Write the word on the line.

wizard	indefinitely	carbon	inventor
current	horseshoe	cheaply	intense
furnish	platinum		

1. An _____ is someone who creates new things.

2. Thomas Edison was called a _____ because he was so clever and created so many new things.

3. Edison wanted to find a way to _____, or supply, people with an easy way to light their homes.

4. He wanted to make his light bulbs _____, so people would not have to pay a lot for them.

5. He was willing to work _____ to find a way to do this.

6. He did not want to use _____, a precious gray metal, because it would cost too much.

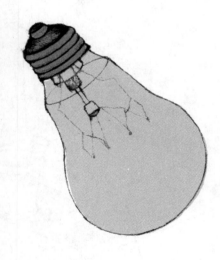

7. He needed a material that would let a strong flow, or _____, of electricity go through the light bulb.

8. He wanted a material that would give off a powerful, or _____, amount of light.

9. He found that _____, a black material left on objects that have been burned, worked best.

10. Do you think he had a U-shaped _____, a symbol of good luck, hanging in his workshop?

ANALOGIES

An **analogy** shows how two words go together in the same way as two other words. A kitten is a baby cat and a puppy is a baby dog. So you could say: <u>Kitten</u> is to <u>cat</u> as <u>puppy</u> is to <u>dog</u>. Write the words from the box to complete the following analogies.

intense	horseshoe	platinum
cheap	inventor	

1. <u>Sneaker</u> is to <u>child</u> as _____ is to <u>horse</u>.

2. <u>Rose</u> is to <u>flower</u> as _____ is to <u>metal</u>.

3. <u>Singer</u> is to <u>sing</u> as _____ is to <u>invent</u>.

4. <u>Weak</u> is to <u>slight</u> as <u>strong</u> is to _____.

5. <u>Good</u> is to <u>bad</u> as _____ is to <u>expensive</u>.

DICTIONARY SKILLS

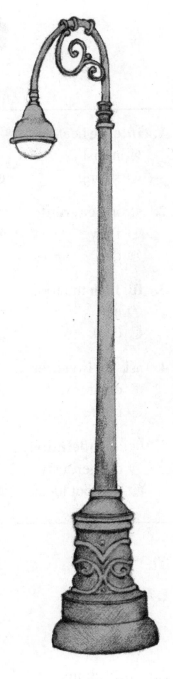

A dictionary can help you find out how to say a word. Turn to page 133 in the Dictionary. Use the **pronunciation key** to help you learn how to say the vocabulary words in ( ) in the sentences below. Write the regular spelling for each word in ( ).

1. You find (kär′bən) after a fire. _____

2. A river can also have a (kûr′ent). _____

3. I will (fûr′nish) apples to eat. _____

4. He may stay (in def′ə nit lē). _____

5. A (wiz′ərd) is a very clever person. _____

15

GET WISE TO TESTS

Directions: Read the phrase. Look for the word or words that have the same or almost the same meaning as the boldfaced word. Mark the answer space for your choice.

Tip — Think about the meaning of the **boldfaced** word before you choose an answer. Don't be fooled by a word that looks like the **boldfaced** word.

1. **intense** heat
   - Ⓐ moist
   - Ⓑ strong
   - Ⓒ weak
   - Ⓓ instant

2. strong **current**
   - Ⓕ flow
   - Ⓖ curl
   - Ⓗ athlete
   - Ⓙ fossil

3. **furnish** the food
   - Ⓐ eat
   - Ⓑ cook
   - Ⓒ supply
   - Ⓓ freeze

4. ask the **inventor**
   - Ⓕ creator
   - Ⓖ pirate
   - Ⓗ insect
   - Ⓙ singer

5. delay **indefinitely**
   - Ⓐ dangerously
   - Ⓑ without ideas
   - Ⓒ sadly
   - Ⓓ without limits

6. **horseshoe** form
   - Ⓕ L-shape
   - Ⓖ Y-shape
   - Ⓗ U-shape
   - Ⓙ T-shape

7. **platinum** wire
   - Ⓐ broken
   - Ⓑ plain
   - Ⓒ glass
   - Ⓓ metal

8. use **carbon**
   - Ⓕ rubber
   - Ⓖ gold
   - Ⓗ control
   - Ⓙ burned material

9. a **wizard**
   - Ⓐ costume
   - Ⓑ clever person
   - Ⓒ willow
   - Ⓓ wild animal

10. bought **cheaply**
    - Ⓕ today
    - Ⓖ at low cost
    - Ⓗ quickly
    - Ⓙ at no cost

Review

1. at **sunset**
   - Ⓐ noon
   - Ⓑ sunrise
   - Ⓒ sundown
   - Ⓓ daylight

2. **daily** chores
   - Ⓕ everyday
   - Ⓖ morning
   - Ⓗ terrible
   - Ⓙ damp

3. his **location**
   - Ⓐ attention
   - Ⓑ position
   - Ⓒ lodging
   - Ⓓ business

4. beautiful **sunrise**
   - Ⓕ twilight
   - Ⓖ evening
   - Ⓗ sunflower
   - Ⓙ dawn

Writing

Imagine that you are Thomas Edison. You have just invented the electric light bulb. Now you want people to buy your light bulbs.

On the lines below, write at least three reasons why your light bulbs are better to use than candles. Use some vocabulary words in your writing.

My light bulbs are better than candles because _____

_____

_____

_____

_____

_____

_____

_____

_____

_____

_____

_____

_____

_____

_____

_____

_____

_____

Turn to "My Word List" on page 131. Write some words from the story or other words that you would like to know more about. Use a dictionary to find the meanings.

★ Read the story below. Think about the meanings of
the **boldfaced** words. ★

Rainbows

A rainbow is an **arch** of colors in the sky. This curved shape is
formed when the sun shines after a **rainstorm**. You can see a
rainbow only at certain times. To **observe** it, you need to have
the sun behind you. The rain must be in front of you.

A rainbow is a **spectacular** sight. It makes people stare in
wonder. A rainbow has six colors — violet, blue, green, yellow,
orange, and red. These colors are also present in sunlight. But
they are very **vivid** in a rainbow. They appear brighter than
usual. *adjective = describer*

A rainbow forms because of what happens when light shines
on water. The sun shines on a **raindrop**. The water **reflects** the
light, or sends it back. The light is broken up into separate
colors.

Of course, the sun shines on many raindrops at once. Each
raindrop breaks the light into the same six colors. Together,
millions of raindrops form a **display** of colors called a rainbow.

Most people have seen rainbows in the sky. But they can
form in other places, too. A rainbow can form wherever light
shines on **moisture**, or wetness. Rainbows sometimes form in
small puddles on the ground. The puddles can be made of
water. But sometimes a rainbow is **visible** in a puddle of oil.
You can also see a rainbow in water that squirts out of a garden
hose.

Next time you see a rainbow, look at the colors. Can you
name them?

★ Go back to the story. Underline the words or sentences that give
you a clue to the meaning of each **boldfaced** word. ★

USING CONTEXT

Meanings for the vocabulary words are given below. Go back to the story and read each sentence that has a vocabulary word. If you still cannot tell the meaning, look for clues in the sentences that come before and after the one with the vocabulary word. Write each word in front of its meaning.

spectacular	observe	moisture	visible
rainstorm	reflects	display	vivid
raindrop	arch		

1. _____: able to be seen

2. _____: a storm with a lot of rain

3. _____: show

4. _____: a single drop of rain

5. _____: very bright

6. _____: striking; amazing

7. _____: a curved shape

8. _____: to watch

9. _____: sends back, as in heat, light, or a picture

10. _____: water in the air

CHALLENGE YOURSELF

Name two things you <u>observe</u> on your way to school.

_____   _____

Name two things that are <u>vivid</u> in color.

_____   _____

19

WORD GROUPS

Read each pair of words. Think about how they are alike. Write the word from the box that best completes each group.

reflects	vivid	arch	moisture
observe	display		

1. curve, loop, _____

2. mirrors, returns, _____

3. watch, notice, _____

4. bright, brilliant, _____

5. water, steam, _____

6. show, exhibit, _____

CLOZE PARAGRAPH

Use the words in the box to complete the paragraph. Reread the paragraph to be sure it makes sense.

display	spectacular	moisture	visible
rainstorm	raindrop		

The air felt damp and full of (1) _____. We went on the picnic anyway. We got the food out. Then I felt one

(2) _____ fall on my head. Seconds later, a

(3) _____ was showering water on us. When it

was over, we saw a (4) _____ of colors in the

sky. A rainbow was (5) _____. The storm

ruined our picnic, but it treated us to a (6) _____ sight!

Directions: Read each sentence carefully. Then choose the best answer to complete each sentence. Mark the space for the answer you have chosen.

Tip Some tests have letters inside the answer circles. Fill in the circle next to your answer, covering the letter, too.

1. When a **rainstorm** is reported, you know there are _____.
   Ⓐ snows   Ⓒ showers
   Ⓑ droughts   Ⓓ suns

2. A **spectacular** movie is one that you will _____.
   Ⓕ ignore   Ⓗ forget
   Ⓖ buy   Ⓙ remember

3. A **vivid** painting has colors that are _____.
   Ⓐ boring   Ⓒ bare
   Ⓑ bright   Ⓓ big

4. When you **observe** something, you _____ it.
   Ⓕ touch   Ⓗ watch
   Ⓖ break   Ⓙ smell

5. **Moisture** in a cellar will make it _____.
   Ⓐ dry   Ⓒ dark
   Ⓑ damp   Ⓓ glow

6. An **arch** is a _____.
   Ⓕ curve   Ⓗ flag
   Ⓖ color   Ⓙ name

7. A **visible** object is one that can be _____.
   Ⓐ heard   Ⓒ seen
   Ⓑ tasted   Ⓓ walked

8. If a **raindrop** lands on you, you become _____.
   Ⓕ visible   Ⓗ happy
   Ⓖ sleepy   Ⓙ wet

9. When an object **reflects** light, the light _____.
   Ⓐ melts   Ⓒ goes home
   Ⓑ disappears   Ⓓ comes back

10. A **display** of art could be a _____ of paintings.
   Ⓕ collection   Ⓗ house
   Ⓖ bucket   Ⓙ city

Writing

A rainbow is not the only beautiful sight you can see in the sky. A sunrise can also be colorful, and so can a sunset. A full moon or a starry sky can also catch your attention.

Compare a rainbow to one of these other sky sights. Explain how they are alike and how they are different. Think about things such as how they look and what time of day you see them. Also think about how often you see them and how long they stay in the sky. Use the pictures and facts from the story to help you. Use some vocabulary words in your writing.

_____

_____

_____

_____

_____

_____

_____

_____

_____

_____

_____

_____

_____

_____

Turn to "My Word List" on page 131. Write some words from the story or other words that you would like to know more about. Use a dictionary to find the meanings.

★ Read the story below. Think about the meanings of the **boldfaced** words. ★

Lights! Lasers! Action!

Brightly colored beams of light fly through the air. Some of them form shapes such as circles and triangles. Others form more lifelike images. They make **realistic** pictures of people and animals. Welcome to a laser light show!

Lasers are tools that **produce** very powerful beams of light. The light that a laser makes is so strong that it can cut a diamond. What makes laser light so powerful? It is very narrow, so it doesn't spread out as it travels. Doctors use lasers. For example, a **physician** can use the beam to cut like a knife. Businesses use them to power machines. In light shows, lasers also have an **artistic** use. They are used to create beauty.

The first laser light show took place in 1973 in the United States. Since then, people have been held **spellbound** by the colors and patterns in these displays. They find it difficult to take their eyes away from the magical beams. In today's laser light shows, the people who control the lasers often **focus** the beams on a wall. Aiming the beam at the wall **transforms** it into a movie screen for laser light pictures. Sometimes the laser **operators** direct the light at mirrors placed around the area. Each mirror reflects the beam onto another mirror for a dazzling effect.

Laser light shows can be found at many theme parks, plays, and sporting events. People around the world **marvel** at the exciting displays. They are filled with wonder as a dark sky suddenly comes alive with dancing lights. Laser light shows **impress** everyone who watches them. They leave people amazed by their magic.

★ Go back to the story. Underline the words or sentences that give you a clue to the meaning of each **boldfaced** word. ★

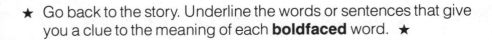

CONTEXT CLUES

Read each sentence. Look for clues to help you complete each sentence with a word from the box. Write the word on the line.

physician	focus	operators	artistic
spellbound	transforms	realistic	produce
marvel	impress		

1. Lasers are machines that _____ very strong beams of light.

2. A _____ can use a laser beam to cut like a knife.

3. The people who create laser light shows use their _____ talents to create beautiful pictures.

4. In a laser light show, laser beams can be used to create very _____ pictures of people.

5. The people who create shows with laser lights can _____ the beams on walls and mirrors.

6. Laser light directed at a wall _____, or changes, the wall into a movie screen.

7. Many people _____ at the light and color created by laser beams.

8. Some people are so _____ by laser light shows that they stare at the designs for a long time.

9. The job of laser _____ is to control the beams.

10. The magical light and color of a laser light show are sure to _____ anyone!

REWRITING SENTENCES

Rewrite each sentence using one of the vocabulary words.

produce	physician	transforms

1. You should see a doctor about that cut on your knee.

   _____

2. In this fairy tale, the kiss from a princess changes a frog into a prince.

   _____

3. Our town has a factory that uses iron to make steel.

   _____

MULTIPLE MEANINGS

The words in the box have more than one meaning. Look for clues in each sentence to tell which meaning is being used. Write the letter of the meaning next to the correct sentence.

impress	produce	focus
a. make a mark on	**a.** fresh fruit and vegetables	**a.** concentrate
b. amaze	**b.** to bring forth	**b.** aim light beams

_____ 1. We can impress the wax because it is soft.

_____ 2. A great movie will impress many people.

_____ 3. A hamster can produce babies every eight weeks.

_____ 4. We bought produce and meat at the grocery store.

_____ 5. Tonight I need to focus on my homework.

_____ 6. You can use a magnifying glass to focus sunlight.

FINE ARTS
BRIGHT LIGHTS
LESSON 4

ANALOGIES

Remember that an **analogy** shows how two words go together in the same way as two other words. Write the words from the box to complete the following analogies.

impress	marvel	artistic	produce

1. Know is to understand as _____ *marvel* _____ is to wonder.

2. Whisper is to yell as _____ is to destroy.

3. Musical is to music as _____ is to artist.

4. Scare is to frighten as _____ is to amaze.

DICTIONARY SKILLS

Write the words in alphabetical order, one word one each line. Then turn to the Dictionary, beginning on page 133. Find each word in the Dictionary. Write its meaning below.

physician	spellbound	focus	transforms
operators	realistic	artistic	impress

1. _____

2. _____

3. _____

4. _____

5. _____

6. _____

7. _____

8. _____

GET WISE TO TESTS

Directions: Fill in the space for the word that fits best in the sentence.

 Tip Read the first sentence carefully. It will help you choose the missing word in the second sentence.

1. My uncle wants to practice medicine. He plans to be a _____.
   Ⓐ physician   Ⓒ coach
   Ⓑ lawyer   Ⓓ child

2. Sara drew a lifelike picture of her mother. It looked very _____.
   Ⓕ green   Ⓗ messy
   Ⓖ realistic   Ⓙ tired

3. That is an auto factory. It can _____ many cars each day.
   Ⓐ laugh   Ⓒ produce
   Ⓑ drive   Ⓓ grow

4. Those people control the machines. They are the _____.
   Ⓕ persons   Ⓗ doctors
   Ⓖ actors   Ⓙ operators

5. I can't find my way in the dark. Please _____ the flashlight over here.
   Ⓐ focus   Ⓒ remove
   Ⓑ break   Ⓓ finish

6. The campers are surprised to see so many stars. They _____ at the sight.
   Ⓕ stop   Ⓗ marvel
   Ⓖ match   Ⓙ sleep

7. The boy drew and painted all the posters for the show. He has a lot of _____ talent.
   Ⓐ weak   Ⓒ mechanical
   Ⓑ artistic   Ⓓ awful

8. That movie is the best one I have ever seen. It will really _____ you.
   Ⓕ sadden   Ⓗ impress
   Ⓖ annoy   Ⓙ bore

9. The new coat of paint makes a big change. It _____ this room.
   Ⓐ chooses   Ⓒ builds
   Ⓑ cleans   Ⓓ transforms

10. I could hardly move when I heard the music. I was _____ by the melody.
    Ⓕ wakened   Ⓗ spellbound
    Ⓖ framed   Ⓙ lost

Review

1. The painting is very bright. It has _____ colors.
   Ⓐ purple   Ⓒ vivid
   Ⓑ angry   Ⓓ dull

2. We watched in amazement. It was a _____ sunset.
   Ⓕ late   Ⓗ normal
   Ⓖ silent   Ⓙ spectacular

Turn to "My Word List" on page 131. Write some words from the story or other words that you would like to know more about. Use a dictionary to find the meanings.

Writing

Suppose that you can create your own laser light show. You can decide where to have it. You can also choose the colors and shapes to use and the pictures to show. You can tell a story. You can make the lights change quickly or slowly.

On the lines below, tell about your laser light show. Use some vocabulary words in your writing.

_____

_____

_____

_____

_____

_____

_____

_____

_____

_____

_____

_____

_____

_____

_____

★ To review the words in Lessons 1–4, turn to page 125. ★

CYCLES OF CHANGE

It is autumn, and this maple tree will soon lose its leaves. It will be bare in the winter. What will happen next in the maple tree's cycle of change?

In Lessons 5 - 8, you will read about growth and change. Think about what grows and changes. A silkworm changes into a moth. A seed becomes a plant. We change, too. Write your ideas on the lines below.

Begins As	Changes To
_____	_____
_____	_____
_____	_____
_____	_____
_____	_____

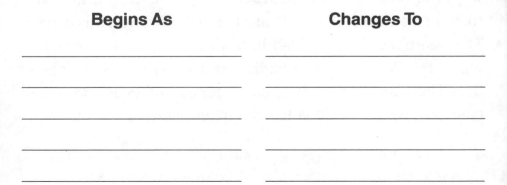

★ Read the story below. Think about the meanings of the **boldfaced** words. ★

An Island Is Born

Before 1963, there was no Surtsey Island. Then one day, Surtsey came right out of the ocean! Many islands are formed in this way as volcanoes grow on the ocean floor.

What is a volcano? And how does one form an island? It starts deep inside the earth. There, the heat is so great that, like a giant **furnace**, it melts rock. This **molten** rock joins with gases and rises up under the ground. If the push upward is great enough, it can make an opening in the earth's surface. Because so much of the earth is covered by oceans, many of these openings appear under the water.

When a volcano **erupts**, the melted rock is thrown up into the water. This **lava** drops back to the ocean floor. There it cools into rock again. And slowly it builds a mountain. As more melted rock is thrown out, it flows down the sides of the mountain. Hard rock is formed on these **slopes**, building up land that grows higher as it spreads wider. Finally, after what may take many years, the mountain reaches the water's surface. It seems to appear suddenly as a tiny island. Still the hot rock **overflows** onto the top of the mountain, adding more land above the water.

In time, the island grows large enough for many people to settle on it. Some of the Hawaiian Islands were formed this way. The volcano may remain **active**, spitting fire and melted rock. In that case, the people must learn to live with this danger. They learn the signs, or **warnings**, that tell when the volcano will erupt. When they feel rumblings in the earth, the people **flee**. They run to find **refuge** on a safer part of the island. There they must wait until the volcano is quiet again.

★ Go back to the story. Underline the words or sentences that give you a clue to the meaning of each **boldfaced** word. ★

USING CONTEXT

Meanings for the vocabulary words are given below. Go back to the story and read each sentence that has a vocabulary word. If you still cannot tell the meaning, look for clues in the sentences that come before and after the one with the vocabulary word. Write each word in front of its meaning.

molten	refuge	active	overflows
furnace	lava	slopes	warnings
erupts	flee		

1. _____: melted rock from a volcano

2. _____: signals or signs that tell of danger

3. _____: a closed-in space in which heat is produced

4. _____: melted by heat

5. _____: to run away from danger

6. _____: working; showing action

7. _____: sides of hills or mountains

8. _____: a place that provides protection

9. _____: runs over the top or brim

10. _____: bursts out; releases suddenly

CHALLENGE YOURSELF

Name two warnings you might hear on a weather report.

_____   _____

Volcanoes are active, but so are you. Name two active things you do.

_____   _____

SYNONYMS

Remember that **synonyms** are words that have the same or almost the same meaning. Match the words in the box with their synonyms listed below. Write each word on the line.

overflows	refuge	erupts	warning

1. caution _~~warning~~_

2. floods _~~overflows~~_

3. explodes _~~erupts~~_

4. shelter _~~refuge~~_

DICTIONARY SKILLS

Guide words are the two words at the top of each dictionary page. They show the first and last entries on that page. All the word entries in between are in alphabetical order. Look at the pairs of guide words. On the lines below each pair, write the words from the box that would appear on the same dictionary page. Be sure to put them in alphabetical order.

slopes	active	lava	furnace
flee	molten		

ability / game	lady / sudden
1. _____	4. _____
2. _____	5. _____
3. _____	6. _____

CROSSWORD PUZZLE

Use the clues and the words in the box to complete the crossword puzzle.

erupts	warnings	flee	furnace	active
refuge	molten	lava	slopes	overflows

Across

2. to run away
6. melted rock
7. on the go
8. hillsides
9. safe place

Down

1. spills over
2. a very hot place
3. blows up
4. melted by heat
5. danger signals

GET WISE TO TESTS

Directions: Fill in the space for the word or words that have the same or almost the same meaning as the boldfaced word.

 Think about the meaning of the **boldfaced** word before you choose an answer. Don't be fooled by a word that looks like the **boldfaced** word.

1. **active** player
   - Ⓐ actual
   - Ⓒ sleeping
   - Ⓑ working
   - Ⓓ huge

2. sudden **warnings**
   - Ⓕ tears
   - Ⓗ songs
   - Ⓖ warriors
   - Ⓙ signals

3. seeks **refuge**
   - Ⓐ repair
   - Ⓒ gifts
   - Ⓑ shelter
   - Ⓓ people

4. **molten** rock
   - Ⓕ magic
   - Ⓗ black
   - Ⓖ cooled
   - Ⓙ melted

5. metal **furnace**
   - Ⓐ heating space
   - Ⓒ watering place
   - Ⓑ cooling space
   - Ⓓ furniture

6. hot **lava**
   - Ⓕ dirt
   - Ⓗ melted rock
   - Ⓖ lace
   - Ⓙ small rocks

7. volcano **erupts**
   - Ⓐ explodes
   - Ⓒ quiets
   - Ⓑ hardens
   - Ⓓ escapes

8. **flee** danger
   - Ⓕ go toward
   - Ⓗ weed out
   - Ⓖ run from
   - Ⓙ fight

9. mountain **slopes**
   - Ⓐ spirits
   - Ⓒ goats
   - Ⓑ insects
   - Ⓓ sides

10. lake **overflows**
    - Ⓕ floods
    - Ⓗ heats
    - Ⓖ colors
    - Ⓙ outruns

Review

1. **focus** the light
   - Ⓐ see
   - Ⓒ aim
   - Ⓑ color
   - Ⓓ darken

2. **transforms** the room
   - Ⓕ tramples
   - Ⓗ likes
   - Ⓖ changes
   - Ⓙ lives in

3. see a **physician**
   - Ⓐ doctor
   - Ⓒ plumber
   - Ⓑ lawyer
   - Ⓓ banker

4. **spellbound** audience
   - Ⓕ splendid
   - Ⓗ angry
   - Ⓖ fascinated
   - Ⓙ bored

Writing

Imagine that you are on vacation in Hawaii. You go to visit Mauna Loa, the biggest volcano. Just as you are about to take a picture, the mountain rumbles. You escape to safety, but you are close enough to see the volcano erupt.

Write an article for the school newspaper telling about your adventure. Describe what you saw and heard when the volcano erupted. Use the picture to help you include details. Use some vocabulary words in your writing.

_____

_____

_____

_____

_____

_____

_____

_____

_____

_____

_____

_____

_____

_____

_____

_____

_____

Turn to "My Word List" on page 131. Write some words from the story or other words that you would like to know more about. Use a dictionary to find the meanings.

★ Read the story below. Think about the meanings of the **boldfaced** words. ★

The Mango Tree

In this legend from India, a girl shows a special kind of love for her brother and her mango tree.

In a small town, there was a small house in which lived a young man, his wife, and the young man's sister. This small house had a small garden at the back in which grew a small **mango** tree. One day the young man's wife came to him and said, "Look here, I'm fed up with our situation."

"Have you come to complain about my sister again? Don't go on," said the brother. "I've heard it all before."

"And what does your lazy sister do all day? Nothing. She lolls about in the garden, watering her mango tree, talking to it, clearing away dead leaves, and feeding it **mulch**."

"That isn't all she does. She comes in and talks to me."

"Just because she **adores** you, doesn't mean you should **ignore** her faults. You must tell her to leave that silly mango tree alone, and come and help me with the housework. I really think we should marry her off."

A marriage was arranged. When all the ceremonies were over, and the sister was about to leave with her groom to lead a new life in a new town, she turned to her sister-in-law and said, "Dearest sister-in-law, I'm going to miss my mango tree so much. Would you please do me a great favor and look after it for me?"

"Oh, well, yes, yes," answered the sister-in-law.

Once the sister had left, the sister-in-law turned to her husband and yelled, "Did you hear that? She didn't say that she was going to miss you. She didn't say that she was going to miss me." The sister-in-law decided then that she was going to ignore the mango tree. Now she could be rid of both.

As the days passed, the unwatered, uncared for mango tree started drying up and its leaves began to fall.

At the same time, the brother, who had been a strong, **robust** and healthy young man, began to lose his **appetite** and get thinner and weaker.

One day a letter arrived. It was from the sister and said, "I hope all is well and that my tree is green and that my brother is in good health."

The remaining leaves of the mango tree were quite yellow by this time, but the sister-in-law wrote back, "Dearest sister. Your tree is fine, but your brother has not been feeling so good."

Soon another letter arrived from the sister. "Are you sure my tree is green? And how is my brother?"

The mango tree had only one brown leaf left on it now, and the brother was so sick that the doctors had said that he could not live. So the sister-in-law wrote back, "Your tree is fine, but the doctors have given up all hopes for your brother."

When the sister received this letter, she raced back to her small **hometown** and went straight into the small garden to water her tree. As she watered, cleared the weeds around it, and mulched it, it began slowly to turn green.

The brother, too, began to **recover**.

As more leaves returned to the tree, the brother's cheeks got pinker and his eyes became brighter. Within a month, the tree was healthy and strong.

And so was the brother.

It was only then that the sister turned to her sister-in-law and said, "Now do you understand? It was not the tree that I loved, but my brother. It was not the tree whose **welfare** I was concerned with, but my brother's. The tree and my brother share a common **soul**. It was my duty to look after them both.

From Seasons of Splendour:
Tales, Myths & Legends of
India, by Madhur Jaffrey

★ Go back to the story. Underline any words or sentences that give you clues to the meanings of the **boldfaced** words. ★

CONTEXT CLUES

Read each sentence. Look for clues to help you complete each sentence with a word from the box. Write the word on the line.

hometown	recover	welfare	appetite
robust	ignore	soul	adores
mango	mulch		

1. A _____ is a kind of fruit.

2. A mango tree needs _____, a covering of straw, leaves, and the like, to grow well.

3. The sister believes the tree and her brother share the same spirit or _____.

4. She _____ her brother, but she shows her love by caring for the tree.

5. She cares about her brother's _____ and wants him to be healthy and happy.

6. She would never _____ the tree, because not paying attention to it would hurt her brother.

7. Her brother loses his _____ and doesn't want to eat when the tree is not fed.

8. Her healthy, _____ brother becomes very ill.

9. She rushes back to her _____, the place where she lived as a child.

10. She helps her brother _____, or get back, his health by caring for the mango tree.

MULTIPLE MEANINGS

The words in the box have more than one meaning. Look for clues in each sentence to tell which meaning is being used. Write the letter of the meaning next to the correct sentence.

soul	appetite	recover
a. a person's spirit	**a.** longing for food	**a.** get back
b. a person	**b.** wish for something	**b.** make up for

_____ **1.** There was not a <u>soul</u> around the old house.

_____ **2.** Those words come from his <u>soul</u>.

_____ **3.** He has such an <u>appetite</u>, he could eat a horse!

_____ **4.** She has an <u>appetite</u> for travel, but not the money.

_____ **5.** Can you <u>recover</u> the lost time by studying more?

_____ **6.** Did the police <u>recover</u> the money stolen from her?

CLASSIFYING

Write each word from the box in the group where it belongs.

welfare	hometown	ignore	mulch
robust	adore	mango	

Plant words _____ _____

Health words _____ _____

Action word _____

Place word _____

Feeling word _____

GET WISE TO TESTS

Directions: Read each sentence carefully. Then choose the best answer to complete each sentence. Mark the space for the answer you have chosen.

 Tip If you are not sure which word completes the sentence, do the best you can. Try to choose the answer that makes the most sense.

1. To **recover** is to _____ your good health.
   - Ⓐ lose
   - Ⓑ get back
   - Ⓒ forget
   - Ⓓ get out

2. An **appetite** is a longing for _____.
   - Ⓕ food
   - Ⓖ sleep
   - Ⓗ light
   - Ⓙ quiet

3. **Mulch** is used in a _____.
   - Ⓐ garden
   - Ⓑ bedroom
   - Ⓒ lake
   - Ⓓ window

4. When someone **adores** you, the person _____ you.
   - Ⓕ hates
   - Ⓖ bakes
   - Ⓗ angers
   - Ⓙ loves

5. If you **ignore** someone, you do not pay _____ to him.
   - Ⓐ dimes
   - Ⓑ cake
   - Ⓒ attention
   - Ⓓ socks

6. A **mango** is a kind of _____.
   - Ⓕ dog
   - Ⓖ dance
   - Ⓗ fruit
   - Ⓙ meat

7. Your **hometown** is the place where you _____.
   - Ⓐ run
   - Ⓑ drive by
   - Ⓒ grow up
   - Ⓓ vacation

8. A **robust** person is _____.
   - Ⓕ wealthy
   - Ⓖ healthy
   - Ⓗ sickly
   - Ⓙ deadly

9. The **soul** is the spirit of _____.
   - Ⓐ money
   - Ⓑ time
   - Ⓒ color
   - Ⓓ life

10. A person who worries about your **welfare** cares about your _____.
    - Ⓕ dog
    - Ⓖ health and happiness
    - Ⓗ flowers
    - Ⓙ songs and dance

Writing

In "The Mango Tree," the sister is concerned about her brother's welfare. She shows her concern by caring for the mango tree.

On the lines below, describe a time when you were concerned about someone's welfare. Tell what you did to show your concern. Use some vocabulary words in your writing.

_____

_____

_____

_____

_____

_____

Turn to "My Word List" on page 131. Write some words from the story or other words that you would like to know more about. Use a dictionary to find the meanings.

_____

_____

_____

41

★ Read the story below. Think about the meanings of the **boldfaced** words. ★

From Tadpole to Frog

Did you know that there are more than 2,000 types of frogs? Some live on or near water all the time. Others **inhabit** land. They live there most of their lives.

People who study animals are called **biologists**. They have found that one thing is the same about all frogs. Each begins as a tadpole. The tadpole is one stage in a frog's **development**. It follows the egg stage.

A tadpole is not fully formed when it hatches. This is an early stage of its **growth**. It lives in the water. Most tadpoles can be found in **lagoons**. Some live in other quiet bodies of water.

The tadpole breathes through **gills**. It is like a fish. In some ways it is more like a fish than like a land animal. That is why water is the best **environment** for it to live in at this stage of its life.

The tadpole's body goes through slow, **gradual** changes as it grows. First, the tail gets longer. Then the tadpole can swim. It **darts** around in the water, moving quickly to find food. It eats underwater plants called **algae**.

Soon, the tadpole's body grows legs. At this point, it also loses its gills. It does all its breathing on land. The tadpole can do this because its gills have been replaced by lungs.

The last change for the tadpole has to do with its tail. When it first hatches, the tail is the longest part of its body. Over time, the tail gets shorter and shorter. Soon, the tail is gone, and the animal becomes a frog.

★ Go back to the story. Underline the words or sentences that give you a clue to the meaning of each **boldfaced** word. ★

CONTEXT CLUES

Read each sentence. Choose a word from the box that means the same as the underlined part of each sentence. Write the word on the line after the sentence.

gills	development	growth	lagoons
inhabit	environment	algae	darts
gradual	biologists		

1. Scientists who <u>study animals</u> sort the frog family into two groups, frogs and toads. _____

2. Most frogs are found in <u>shallow bodies of water</u>. _____

3. Toads <u>live in</u> dry places on land. _____

4. A frog's <u>natural changes caused by growing</u> are interesting. _____

5. In one stage of <u>the process of growing</u>, a frog is called a tadpole. _____

6. It has <u>breathing organs</u> in its head. _____

7. It feeds on <u>underwater plants</u>. _____

8. <u>Slow but steady</u> changes happen as the tadpole grows larger. _____

9. Now it <u>moves quickly</u> everywhere. _____

10. In this friendly <u>setting</u>, a tadpole will grow into a frog. _____

CHALLENGE YOURSELF

Name two animals that <u>inhabit lagoons</u>.

_____   _____

SCIENCE WORDS

The words in the box all have to do with the science that studies plant and animal life. Write each word beside its meaning.

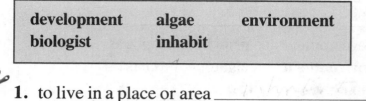

development	algae	environment
biologist	inhabit	

1. to live in a place or area _____ *inhabit* ✓

2. small plants found underwater _____ *algae*

3. natural stages in growing _____ *developmental stor*

4. surroundings that affect living things _____ *environment*

5. person who studies animal and
   plant life _____ *Biologist*

ANALOGIES

Remember that an **analogy** shows how two words go together in the same way as two other words. Write the words from the box to complete the following analogies.

growth	lagoons	gills	gradual	darts

1. Lungs are to people as _____ are to fish.

2. Hills are to dirt as _____ are to water.

3. Runs is to horse as _____ *darts* is to tadpole.

4. Slow is to fast as _____ *gradual* is to sudden.

5. Build is to house as _____ *growth* is to person.

Directions: Read each sentence. Pick the word that best completes the sentence. Mark the letter for that word.

Tip Read carefully. Use the other words in the sentence to help you choose the missing word.

1. Some frogs _____ small ponds.
   - Ⓐ dig
   - Ⓒ tadpole
   - Ⓑ inhabit
   - Ⓓ bury

2. _____ study frogs.
   - Ⓕ Jump
   - Ⓗ Biologists
   - Ⓖ Science
   - Ⓙ Plants

3. The process is slow and _____.
   - Ⓐ hatch
   - Ⓒ quickly
   - Ⓑ gone
   - Ⓓ gradual

4. Fish breathe through _____.
   - Ⓕ gills
   - Ⓗ nothing
   - Ⓖ watering
   - Ⓙ biologists

5. A pond is a good _____ for a frog.
   - Ⓐ inhabit
   - Ⓒ homely
   - Ⓑ station
   - Ⓓ environment

6. Frogs like ponds and _____.
   - Ⓕ dances
   - Ⓗ darts
   - Ⓖ lagoons
   - Ⓙ cities

7. _____ is the process of getting larger.
   - Ⓐ Growth
   - Ⓒ Remembering
   - Ⓑ Death
   - Ⓓ Go

8. Tadpoles eat _____.
   - Ⓕ shell
   - Ⓗ nothing
   - Ⓖ quickly
   - Ⓙ algae

9. A frog's _____ is how it changes.
   - Ⓐ friend
   - Ⓒ development
   - Ⓑ follows
   - Ⓓ environments

10. When a fish _____, it moves quickly.
    - Ⓕ creeps
    - Ⓗ swimming
    - Ⓖ pond
    - Ⓙ darts

Review

1. He is strong and _____.
   - Ⓐ weak
   - Ⓒ happily
   - Ⓑ robust
   - Ⓓ soul

2. We visited my mother's _____.
   - Ⓕ appetite
   - Ⓗ hometown
   - Ⓖ friendly
   - Ⓙ oceans

3. She will _____ her health.
   - Ⓐ locate
   - Ⓒ lost
   - Ⓑ ignoring
   - Ⓓ recover

4. A _____ is a kind of fruit.
   - Ⓕ mango
   - Ⓗ cry
   - Ⓖ carrot
   - Ⓙ mulch

Writing

Did you know that a butterfly is like a frog in some ways? A butterfly also begins life looking completely different from the way it looks when it is full-grown. A butterfly begins as a tiny egg. The egg hatches into a caterpillar. The caterpillar eats lots of leaves. When it is time, the caterpillar spins a kind of shell around itself. After many days, a butterfly comes out of this shell.

Use the story and the pictures on this page to compare a butterfly to a frog. Think about how they are alike and different. Use some vocabulary words in your writing.

A frog and a butterfly both begin their lives as tiny

eggs. _____

_____

_____

_____

_____

_____

_____

_____

_____

_____

_____

_____

_____

_____

Turn to "My Word List" on page 131. Write some words from the story or other words that you would like to know more about. Use a dictionary to find the meanings.

★ Read the story below. Think about the meanings of the **boldfaced** words. ★

How Does Your Skin Grow?

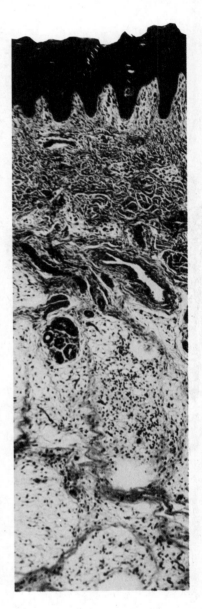

As you grow, your skin grows, too. In fact, throughout your **lifetime** your skin keeps growing. Stare at your arm for about 60 seconds. Can you see any change? Probably not. Now, with your fingernail, gently **scrape** the surface of your skin. What you see are tiny specks that are flakes of skin cells. This is quite **normal**. Every hour your body sheds about one million dead skin cells.

Skin is strong and tough. It protects the muscles and organs underneath. It also keeps dangerous germs from entering the body. What keeps your skin strong? Do you know how your skin grows?

Skin is made up of three layers. Each layer has a **function**, or a different job to do. The bottom layer is thick and holds sweat **glands** and **nerves**, which help you feel. The sweat glands **insulate**, or keep the body from getting too hot. Cells in the glands make sweat. Sweat reaches the surface of the skin and dries, keeping you cool.

The middle layer of your skin has millions of cells. These cells grow and divide into other cells. As new cells are made, some are pushed to the top layer. The cells pushed to the surface are dead skin cells. The dead layer of skin rubs off. Then a new layer of skin takes its place. This keeps your skin **healthy**. Your skin keeps growing this way even as a **mature** adult.

Imagine, every month you have an almost completely new outer skin! It would be truly amazing to watch this change happen. But the growth and change of skin is **invisible** to the naked eye.

★ Go back to the story. Underline the words or sentences that give you a clue to the meaning of each **boldfaced** word. ★

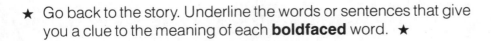

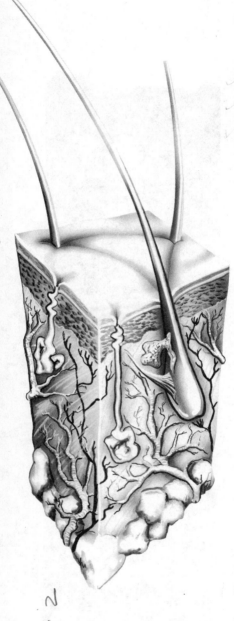

USING CONTEXT

Meanings for the vocabulary words are given below. Go back to the story and read each sentence that has a vocabulary word. If you still cannot tell the meaning, look for clues in the sentences that come before and after the one with the vocabulary word. Write each word in front of its meaning.

lifetime	healthy	invisible	insulate
glands	mature	function	scrape
nerves	normal		

1. _____ : the length of a person's life

2. _____ : to scratch from the surface

3. _____ : usual condition

4. _____ : groups of cells that alert the body to feel heat, cold, and pain

5. _____ : purpose

6. _____ : organs that produce materials used by the body

7. _____ : to protect something from getting too hot or too cold

8. _____ : well; fit

9. _____ : not able to be seen

10. _____ : full-grown; developed

CHALLENGE YOURSELF

Name two things you can do to keep your skin <u>healthy</u>.

Name two things that <u>insulate</u> your body from the cold.

_____ _____

SYNONYMS

Synonyms are words that have the same or almost the same meaning. Match the words in the box with their synonyms listed below. Write each word on the line.

| invisible | scrape | healthy |
| function | normal | mature |

1. usual _____
2. job _____
3. unseen _____
4. fit _____
5. full-grown _____
6. scratch _____

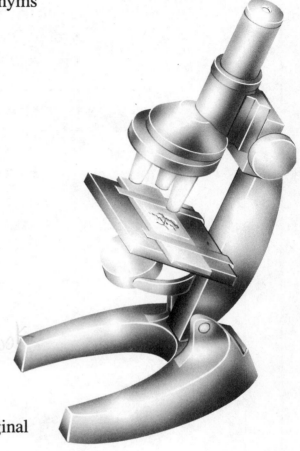

WRITING SENTENCES

Use each vocabulary word in the box to write an original sentence.

| insulate | mature | nerves |
| lifetime | glands | healthy |

1. _____
2. _____
3. _____
4. _____
5. _____
6. _____

WORD MAP

Use the vocabulary words in the box to complete the word map about the human body. Add other words that you know to each group. One heading will not have any vocabulary words, but only your words.

mature	normal	glands	healthy	nerves

Parts of the Body

1. _____
2. _____
3. _____
4. _____
5. _____

How a Body Can Look

1. _____
2. _____
3. _____
4. _____
5. _____

THE HUMAN BODY

What a Body Can Do

1. _____
2. _____
3. _____
4. _____
5. _____

Directions: Read the phrase. Look for the word or words that have the same or almost the same meaning as the boldfaced word. Mark the answer space for your choice.

 Think about the meaning of the **boldfaced** word before you choose an answer. Don't be fooled by a word that looks like the **boldfaced** word.

1. sweat **glands**
   - Ⓐ hairs
   - Ⓑ strands
   - Ⓒ organs
   - Ⓓ waters

2. **mature** adult
   - Ⓕ awake
   - Ⓖ happy
   - Ⓗ young
   - Ⓙ full-grown

3. important **function**
   - Ⓐ forecast
   - Ⓑ purpose
   - Ⓒ day
   - Ⓓ success

4. **invisible** star
   - Ⓕ unseen
   - Ⓖ fading
   - Ⓗ interesting
   - Ⓙ valuable

5. **insulate** a house
   - Ⓐ search
   - Ⓑ look for
   - Ⓒ protect
   - Ⓓ inspire

6. **healthy** cat
   - Ⓕ helpless
   - Ⓖ sleepy
   - Ⓗ wealthy
   - Ⓙ well

7. long **lifetime**
   - Ⓐ dream
   - Ⓑ length of life
   - Ⓒ lightning
   - Ⓓ end of life

8. **normal** day
   - Ⓕ usual
   - Ⓖ long
   - Ⓗ northern
   - Ⓙ important

9. **scrape** a knee
   - Ⓐ rest
   - Ⓑ bend
   - Ⓒ scold
   - Ⓓ scratch

10. **nerves** feel
    - Ⓕ nephews
    - Ⓖ body parts
    - Ⓗ plants
    - Ⓙ car parts

Review

1. **inhabit** lakes
   - Ⓐ buy
   - Ⓑ harm
   - Ⓒ involve
   - Ⓓ live in

2. **gradual** change
   - Ⓕ slow
   - Ⓖ great
   - Ⓗ quiet
   - Ⓙ quick

3. animal **darts**
   - Ⓐ walks
   - Ⓑ moves quickly
   - Ⓒ dozes
   - Ⓓ laughs a lot

4. fish **gills**
   - Ⓕ eyes
   - Ⓖ grim looks
   - Ⓗ fins
   - Ⓙ breathing organs

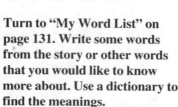

Your skin stays healthy by getting rid of dead cells. There are things that you can do, too, to help keep your skin in good health.

Look at the pictures. Use those ideas and others you have to write rules for taking care of your skin. Use some vocabulary words in your writing.

Rule 1: You should keep your skin healthy by _____

_____

_____

_____

_____

_____

_____

_____

_____

_____

_____

_____

Turn to "My Word List" on page 131. Write some words from the story or other words that you would like to know more about. Use a dictionary to find the meanings.

_____

_____

_____

_____

★ To review the words in Lessons 5–8, turn to page 126. ★

WILD RACES

The race is on. Who will be first to cross the finish line and claim the winner's prize? It takes skill and training to be a champion.

In Lessons 9 - 12, you will read about some unusual races. Imagine racing across the desert sand or snow-covered ground, or through the air to reach the moon. Think about races you have seen or heard about. Write your ideas on the lines below.

Kinds of Races	**Where Races Are Held**
_____	_____
_____	_____
_____	_____
_____	_____
_____	_____

★ Read the story below. Think about the meanings of the **boldfaced** words. ★

The King's Camel Race

Picture 2,500 **camels** racing across the desert. Young Arab boys ride the humped animals, **coaxing** and urging them on. Dust clouds rise in the air. When one camel, then another, breaks out of the pack and **lunges** ahead, people cheer.

This **competition** is called the King's Camel Race. This twelve-mile event takes place every spring outside Riyadh, the capital of Saudi Arabia.

In this part of the world, camels are still very important. They are used for milk and meat and for travel in the desert. And sometimes they are raced like horses.

Because of the big prizes, many people want to win. So there are many **entries** in the race. Hundreds of other people come just to watch the **spectacle**. When the race is over, no one forgets the amazing sight.

Getting ready for the race takes work. The boys feed their camels a special mix of grains. They exercise them every day to prepare for the long race. But riding a camel is not easy. Even after weeks of practice, some boys still fall off their camels. Or they get tired of sitting on the beast and are forced to stop and **dismount**.

The top 200 riders all **qualify** for prizes from the king. But the best prizes go to the rider with the swiftest camel that **outruns** all the others. For this **champion**, the winner of the race, there is a gold dagger, money, and a truck.

★ Go back to the story. Underline the words or sentences that give you a clue to the meaning of each **boldfaced** word. ★

CONTEXT CLUES

Read each sentence. Look for clues to help you complete each
sentence with a word from the box. Write the word on the line.

competition	spectacle	camels	qualify
coaxing	entries	dismount	champion
outruns	lunges		

1. Humped animals called _____ are raced in
   the desert.

2. The Arab boys who enter the _____ are
   serious about winning the race.

3. To _____, or to show to be fit for the race,
   a boy needs a fast camel.

4. There are a great number of _____, or
   people in the contest, because the one and only winner gets
   wonderful prizes.

5. The _____, or winner, of the camel race
   wins a truck!

6. The boy whose camel _____ all the others
   will win.

7. To urge his camel to run faster, a boy might talk to the

   beast, _____ it on.

8. A camel that obeys is the one that _____
   ahead by taking big steps.

9. A camel may stop and force its rider to get down, or

   to _____, during the race.

10. A camel race in the desert is an amazing

    _____!

BASE WORDS

Base words are words without any endings or other word parts added to them. For each word below, write its base word next to it on the line. Remember, sometimes the spelling of the base word changes when an ending is added to it. Turn to the Dictionary, beginning on page 133, if you need help spelling the base words.

1. camels _____

2. coaxing _____

3. dismounted _____

4. entries _____

5. lunges _____

WORD GROUPS

Read each pair of words. Think about how they are alike. Write the word from the box that best completes each group.

spectacle	qualify	champion
competition	lunge	outruns

1. beats, tops, _____

2. contest, meet, _____

3. winner, leader, _____

4. show, display, _____

5. pass, fit, _____

6. leap, spring, _____

WORD PUZZLE

Write a word from the box next to each clue. Then read the words formed by the letters in the squares. You will have the answer to the question below.

To what part of the world would you go to see the King's

Camel Race? The _____ _____

camel	lunges	entries	competition
outruns	coaxed	champion	spectacle
qualify	dismount		

1. the winner _ _ _ □ _ _ _ _

2. those taking part in a contest _ _ _ _ □ _ _

3. to get off □ _ _ _ _ _ _ _

4. urged on _ _ _ _ _ □

5. moves forward suddenly □ _ _ _ _ _

6. contest; race _ _ _ _ □ _ _ _ _ _

7. a desert animal _ _ _ □ _

8. show to have the needed ability _ _ □ _ _ _ _

9. goes faster than others _ _ _ _ _ _ □

10. an amazing show _ _ _ _ □ _ _ _ _

Directions: Read each sentence. Pick the word that best completes the sentence. Mark the letter for that word.

 Tip Some tests put letters before the answer choices. Be sure to find the letter of the answer you think is correct and then fill in the circle beside it.

1. All _____ have one or two humps.
   Ⓐ riding   Ⓒ elephants
   Ⓑ camels   Ⓓ champion

2. The rider decided to stop and _____.
   Ⓕ drinking   Ⓗ dismount
   Ⓖ races   Ⓙ crossed

3. She finished her work so she will _____ for a prize.
   Ⓐ qualify   Ⓒ speeds
   Ⓑ entries   Ⓓ like

4. The camel _____ ahead and wins.
   Ⓕ quicks   Ⓗ pleasing
   Ⓖ danger   Ⓙ lunges

5. There are two _____ in the race.
   Ⓐ winning   Ⓒ catches
   Ⓑ entries   Ⓓ moon

6. The circus was a big _____.
   Ⓕ crowding   Ⓗ dismount
   Ⓖ spectacle   Ⓙ person

7. The _____ will be held in the gym.
   Ⓐ qualify   Ⓒ outruns
   Ⓑ city   Ⓓ competition

8. She is a _____ skater.
   Ⓕ champion   Ⓗ dirt
   Ⓖ coaxing   Ⓙ icing

9. My horse _____ the others and wins the race.
   Ⓐ laughed   Ⓒ outruns
   Ⓑ kicking   Ⓓ camels

10. He is _____ his dog to roll over.
   Ⓕ champion   Ⓗ refusing
   Ⓖ kitten   Ⓙ coaxing

Review

1. You _____ a house to protect it from the heat and cold.
   Ⓐ insulate   Ⓒ ruin
   Ⓑ painting   Ⓓ mature

2. A person who is very old has had a long _____.
   Ⓕ birth   Ⓗ lifetime
   Ⓖ normal   Ⓙ days

Writing

The champion of the King's Camel Race wins a gold dagger, money, and a truck. Pretend that you are the winner of an auto race or a horse race. You have won a million dollars.

Use the lines below to write about what you would do with your prize money. Use some vocabulary words in your writing.

If I won one million dollars, I would _____

_____

_____

_____

_____

_____

_____

_____

_____

_____

_____

_____

_____

_____

_____

_____

_____

Turn to "My Word List" on page 132. Write some words from the story or other words that you would like to know more about. Use a dictionary to find the meanings.

59

★ Read the story below. Think about the meanings of the **boldfaced** words. ★

The Race

Determined to save his sick grandfather's farm, little Willy and his dog, Searchlight, try to win big prize money. They must outrun the best dogsled racers in the country. That includes the legendary Native American, Stone Fox, and his Samoyed dogs.

"Go, Searchlight! Go!" little Willy sang out. The snow was well packed. It was going to be a fast race today. The road was full of dangerous twists and turns, but little Willy did not have to slow down as the other **racers** did. With only one dog and a small sled, he was able to take the sharp turns at full speed without **risk** of sliding off the road or losing control.

About three miles out of town the road made a half circle around a frozen lake. Instead of following the turn, little Willy took a **shortcut** right across the lake. This was tricky going, but Searchlight had done it many times before.

Little Willy had asked Mayor Smiley if he was **permitted** to go across the lake, not wanting to be disqualified. "As long as you leave town heading north and come back on South Road," the mayor had said, "anything goes!"

None of the other racers **attempted** to cross the lake. Not even Stone Fox. The risk of falling through the ice was just too great.

Little Willy's lead increased.

At the end of five miles, little Willy was so far out in front that he couldn't see anybody behind him when he looked back.

He knew, however, that the return five miles, going back into town, would not be this easy. The trail along South Road was practically straight and very smooth, and Stone Fox was sure to close the **gap**.

Grandfather's farm was coming up.

When Searchlight saw the farmhouse, she started to pick up speed. "No, girl," little Willy yelled. "Not yet."

As they approached the farmhouse, little Willy thought he saw someone in Grandfather's bedroom window.

It couldn't be. But it was! It was Grandfather! Grandfather was sitting up in bed. He was looking out the window.

Little Willy was so excited he couldn't think straight. He started to stop the sled, but Grandfather indicated no, waving him on.

"Go, Searchlight!" little Willy **shrieked**. "Go, girl!"

Grandfather was better. Tears of joy rolled down little Willy's smiling face. Everything was going to be all right.

And then Stone Fox made his move. One by one he began to pass the other racers. Until only little Willy remained.

Little Willy still had a good lead. In fact, it was not until the last two miles of the race that Stone Fox got his first **glimpse** of little Willy since the race had begun.

The five Samoyeds looked magnificent as they moved effortlessly across the snow. Stone Fox was **gaining**, and he was gaining fast. And little Willy wasn't aware of it.

Finally little Willy glanced back over his shoulder. He couldn't believe what he saw! Stone Fox was nearly on top of him!

The lead Samoyed passed little Willy and pulled up even with Searchlight. Then it was a nose ahead. But that was all. Searchlight moved forward, inching *her* nose ahead. Then the Samoyed **regained** the lead. Then Searchlight. . .

When you enter the town of Jackson on South Road, the first buildings come into view about a half a mile away. Whether Searchlight took those buildings to be Grandfather's farmhouse again, no one can be sure, but it was at this time that she poured on the steam. Little Willy's sled seemed to lift up off the ground and fly. Stone Fox was left behind.

From Stone Fox, by John Reynolds Gardiner

★ Go back to the story. Underline any words or sentences that give you clues to the meanings of the **boldfaced** words. ★

USING CONTEXT

Meanings for the vocabulary words are given below. Go back to the story and read each sentence that has a vocabulary word. If you still cannot tell the meaning, look for clues in the sentences that come before and after the one with the vocabulary word. Write each word in front of its meaning.

attempted	permitted	gaining	gap
racers	shortcut	regained	risk
glimpse	shrieked		

1. _____: a quicker way of doing something or of getting somewhere

2. _____: tried

3. _____: a chance of harm

4. _____: got back again

5. _____: screamed in a high voice

6. _____: a space; an opening

7. _____: coming closer; catching up with

8. _____: a quick look

9. _____: those who run in a competition

10. _____: allowed

CHALLENGE YOURSELF

Name two things that have a <u>gap</u> between them.

_____   _____

Name two sports in which <u>racers</u> compete.

_____   _____

ANTONYMS

Antonyms are words that have opposite meanings. Match the words in the box with their antonyms listed below. Write each word on the line.

permitted	glimpse	risky	gaining

1. stare _____
2. losing _____
3. safe _____
4. refused _____

DICTIONARY SKILLS

An **entry** on a dictionary page is the base form of the word that appears in **boldface** before its meaning. Word endings that can be added to the base word come after the meaning.

Turn to the Dictionary, beginning on page 133. Write each word in the box as it appears as an entry on each dictionary page. Then write the meaning of each word.

attempted	racers	shortcut	shrieked
regained	gap		

1. _____
2. _____
3. _____
4. _____
5. _____
6. _____

GET WISE TO TESTS

Directions: Find the word or words that mean the same, or about the same, as the boldfaced word. Mark your answer.

Tip This test will show you how well you understand the meaning of the words. Think about the meaning of the **boldfaced** word before you choose your answer.

Review

1. **coaxing** her on
   - Ⓐ protecting
   - Ⓑ washing
   - Ⓒ urging
   - Ⓓ scaring

2. to **dismount**
   - Ⓕ get up
   - Ⓖ get down
   - Ⓗ sleep
   - Ⓙ drive

3. grand **spectacle**
   - Ⓐ show
   - Ⓑ car
   - Ⓒ flower
   - Ⓓ food

4. **qualify** to join
   - Ⓕ want
   - Ⓖ show anger
   - Ⓗ forget
   - Ⓙ show to be fit

5. is the **champion**
   - Ⓐ racer
   - Ⓑ winner
   - Ⓒ competition
   - Ⓓ loser

---

1. **gaining** on us
   - Ⓐ claiming
   - Ⓑ fighting
   - Ⓒ coming closer
   - Ⓓ going apart

2. quick **glimpse**
   - Ⓕ look
   - Ⓖ question
   - Ⓗ answer
   - Ⓙ visit

3. **permitted** to go
   - Ⓐ refused
   - Ⓑ pleased
   - Ⓒ forced
   - Ⓓ allowed

4. a great **risk**
   - Ⓕ picture
   - Ⓖ chance
   - Ⓗ pain
   - Ⓙ prize

5. **shrieked** loudly
   - Ⓐ clapped
   - Ⓑ scratched
   - Ⓒ barked
   - Ⓓ screamed

6. **attempted** the jump
   - Ⓕ tried
   - Ⓖ saw
   - Ⓗ raced
   - Ⓙ refused

7. wide **gap**
   - Ⓐ feet
   - Ⓑ cut
   - Ⓒ space
   - Ⓓ nose

8. **racers** are off
   - Ⓕ those who sing
   - Ⓖ those who watch
   - Ⓗ those who run
   - Ⓙ those who wait

9. **regained** the lead
   - Ⓐ remembered
   - Ⓑ got back
   - Ⓒ got lost
   - Ⓓ reported

10. took a **shortcut**
   - Ⓕ funny way
   - Ⓖ longer way
   - Ⓗ cleaner way
   - Ⓙ quicker way

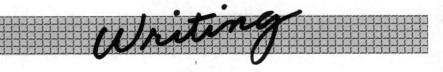

Newspapers often send reporters to write about a race. Imagine that you are a reporter writing about the dogsled race.

Finish the article below. Look at the pictures to help you describe what happened. Remember to tell <u>who</u>, <u>what</u>, <u>where</u>, <u>when</u>, <u>why</u>, and <u>how</u> in your story. Use some vocabulary words in your writing.

Close Contest

Willy and his dog, Searchlight, raced against Stone Fox and

his team of Samoyeds today. _____

_____

_____

_____

_____

_____

_____

_____

_____

_____

_____

Turn to "My Word List" on page 132. Write some words from the story or other words that you would like to know more about. Use a dictionary to find the meanings.

_____

_____

_____

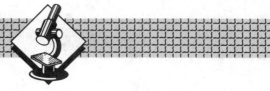

★ Read the story below. Think about the meanings of the **boldfaced** words. ★

The Great Space Race

Some people believe the world's greatest race was the Space Race. The United States and the former Soviet Union raced to see which country would be the first to **conquer** outer space. When did the Space Race start? On October 4, 1957, the Soviet Union sent a **satellite** named Sputnik I into space. This tiny, human-made moon sent radio signals to people in **nations** around the world. The Space Age and the Space Race had begun!

The United States had hoped to **launch** a satellite first. But there was trouble at the American rocket base when a rocket blew up. This caused a long **delay**. The United States did not send up its first satellite until January 31, 1958. So the Soviet Union took the early lead in the Space Race.

People around the globe watched to see which country would be first to send up a **spacecraft** with a person inside. On April 12, 1961, Yuri Gagarin, a Soviet **astronaut**, circled the earth. For the second time, the Soviet Union was **triumphant**. But the United States was very close behind. Just one month later, Alan Shepard became the first American in space.

Then the world wondered which country would be the first to land a rocket with people on board on the moon. The Soviet Union had been ahead. But American scientists pushed hard to catch up. Finally, they jumped ahead. In December 1968, American astronauts **orbited** the moon. Then in July of 1969, two Americans, Neil Armstrong and Edwin Aldrin, walked on the surface of the moon.

Later, both countries built space stations for gathering information. The countries started working together to collect **data** about outer space. Today, Russia and the United States still work together to unlock the mysteries of the stars and more.

★ Go back to the story. Underline the words or sentences that give you a clue to the meaning of each **boldfaced** word. ★

CONTEXT CLUES

Read each sentence. Look for clues to help you complete each sentence with a word from the box. Write the word on the line.

spacecraft	conquer	orbited	astronaut
satellite	delay	nations	launch
triumphant	data		

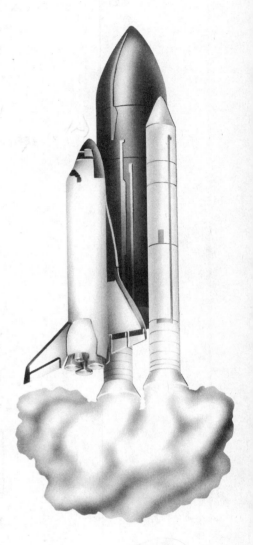

1. Two _____, the United States and the former Soviet Union, competed against one another in the Space Race.

2. They began the world's effort to _____, or win victory over, this unknown region.

3. Each country ran into more than one

   _____ that held up the path to victory.

4. The first step was to send a _____, a human-made moon, into space.

5. At first, it was the former Soviet Union that was

   _____, or successful.

6. Today many countries _____ satellites into space.

7. Some satellites send back _____, or information, about the weather.

8. Satellites have _____, or circled, the earth for many years.

9. It is an exciting event when a _____ with people inside it is sent into outer space.

10. It used to be that an _____ had to be a pilot, but today a scientist or engineer can be one, too.

ANALOGIES

An **analogy** shows how two words go together in the same way as two other words. Write the words from the box to complete the following analogies.

| satellite | spacecraft | delay |
| nation | astronaut | |

1. Diver is to ocean as _____ is to space.

2. Rush is to go as _____ is to stop.

3. Car is to automobile as _____ is to moon.

4. Subway is to underground as _____ is to space.

5. City is to Dallas as _____ is to the United States.

WORD GROUPS

Read each pair of words. Think about how they are alike. Write the word from the box that completes each group.

| nations | triumphant | orbit | data |
| launch | conquer | | |

1. countries, governments, _____

2. send, begin, _____

3. circle, ring, _____

4. facts, information, _____

5. winning, successful, _____

6. defeat, win, _____

GET WISE TO TESTS

Directions: Read each sentence carefully. Then choose the best answer to complete each sentence. Mark the space for the answer you have chosen.

Tip If you are not sure which word completes the sentence, do the best you can. Try to choose the answer that makes the most sense.

1. To **launch** is to _____.
   Ⓐ send off   Ⓒ break down
   Ⓑ clean up   Ⓓ smash up

2. Something that has **orbited** the Earth has _____ it.
   Ⓕ broken   Ⓗ circled
   Ⓖ forgotten   Ⓙ liked

3. A **triumphant** army has been _____.
   Ⓐ defeated   Ⓒ stolen
   Ⓑ successful   Ⓓ forgotten

4. A **spacecraft** is a _____.
   Ⓕ dog   Ⓗ spaceship
   Ⓖ creature   Ⓙ walk

5. The **nations** of the world are the different _____.
   Ⓐ rivers   Ⓒ mountains
   Ⓑ countries   Ⓓ continents

6. An **astronaut** is a _____.
   Ⓕ star   Ⓗ spaceship
   Ⓖ moon   Ⓙ space traveler

7. A **delay** is a _____.
   Ⓐ birth   Ⓒ deal
   Ⓑ wait   Ⓓ dress

8. If you collect **data**, you gather _____.
   Ⓕ stamps   Ⓗ information
   Ⓖ money   Ⓙ food

9. A **satellite** is a _____.
   Ⓐ planet   Ⓒ hand-made lamp
   Ⓑ sun   Ⓓ human-made moon

10. When an army sets out to **conquer** a city, it wants to _____ it.
   Ⓕ win   Ⓗ find
   Ⓖ lose   Ⓙ build

Writing

Being an astronaut can mean having exciting adventures. It can also mean facing the unknown. Would you like to be an astronaut someday? Or would you like to be among the people who may live on a space station someday?

Write a paragraph explaining your feelings about being an astronaut or another kind of space traveler. Support your ideas by explaining why you would or would not like to go into space. Use some vocabulary words in your writing.

Turn to "My Word List" on page 132. Write some words from the story or other words that you would like to know more about. Use a dictionary to find the meanings.

_____

_____

_____

_____

_____

_____

_____

_____

_____

_____

_____

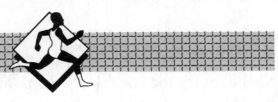

★ Read the story below. Think about the meanings of the **boldfaced** words. ★

Tarahumara Racers

It is race day for the Tarahumara Indians. Their aim is to run a 90-mile race. It will not be easy to meet their **goal**. They must run over a **rugged** mountain course. There are sharp rocks and uneven ground. They will run the course without stopping. Some will even run without shoes. It takes great **determination** to run this race. Each runner needs a strong spirit. There are many hardships to **overcome**. The runners must rise above these difficulties.

The Tarahumara live in the mountains and deep valleys of northern Mexico. Their races are an important part of their lives. The races have been held for hundreds of years. Usually there are two races a year. They celebrate times of harvest in different parts of the country.

Teams of male runners from two villages run against each other. The **opponents** play a ball game as they run. Each one uses the top of a foot to scoop up the ball and throw it. The first player to send the ball over the finish line claims **victory** for his team. His team wins!

How do the runners keep from getting tired on the 15-hour races? Many of them tie deer hooves to their belts. They fight their **weariness** by listening to the sound of the hooves beating together.

Loneliness is not a problem for the runners. There are always other people close by. They offer water to the strong and **hardy** runners. They also carry torches to help runners see at night. In these ways, other village members help the runners **endure** the many hardships of the race. The winners are proud of themselves. And so are the other members of the village.

★ Go back to the story. Underline the words or sentences that give you a clue to the meaning of each **boldfaced** word. ★

USING CONTEXT

Meanings for the vocabulary words are given below. Go back to the story and read each sentence that has a vocabulary word. If you still cannot tell the meaning, look for clues in the sentences that come before and after the one with the vocabulary word. Write each word in front of its meaning.

goal	overcome	determination	rugged
hardy	opponents	loneliness	endure
victory	weariness		

1. _____: wanting to be with others

2. _____: an aim; something wished for

3. _____: put up with

4. _____: the will to go on and not quit

5. _____: people trying to win the same contest

6. _____: tough; able to stand harsh conditions

7. _____: the feeling of being very tired

8. _____: rough and bumpy

9. _____: success

10. _____: conquer; defeat

72

SYNONYMS

Remember that **synonyms** are words that have the same or almost the same meaning. Cross out the word in each line that is not a synonym.

1. rugged   smooth   harsh   rough

2. hardy   strong   healthy   weak

3. endure   continue   end   last

4. overcome   fail   defeat   beat

5. goal   start   aim   purpose

6. victory   failure   win   success

DICTIONARY SKILLS

Write the words in alphabetical order, one word on each line. Then turn to the Dictionary, beginning on page 133. Find each word in the Dictionary. Write its meaning below.

| loneliness | determination | weariness | goal |
| victory | opponents | overcome | hardy |

1. _____

2. _____

3. _____

4. _____

5. _____

6. _____

7. _____

8. _____

ANALOGIES

Remember that an **analogy** shows how two words go together in the same way as two other words. Write the words from the box to complete the following analogies.

opponents	loneliness	determination
victory	weariness	

1. Friend is to enemy as _____ is to defeat.

2. Players is to game as _____ is to contest.

3. Answer is to reply as _____ is to courage.

4. Name is to title as _____weariness_____ is to tiredness.

5. Hunger is to food as _____ is to friend.

WRITING SENTENCES

Use each vocabulary word in the box to write an original sentence.

goal	rugged	opponents
victory	hardy	

1. _____

2. _____

3. _____

4. _____

5. _____

Directions: Read each sentence carefully. Then choose the best answer to complete each sentence. Mark the space for the answer you have chosen.

 Tip Some tests have letters inside the answer circles. Fill in the circle next to your answer, covering the letter, too.

1. Her _____ is to get 100% on the test.
   - Ⓐ school
   - Ⓑ goal
   - Ⓒ hardy
   - Ⓓ better

2. The sharp rocks make this a _____ trail.
   - Ⓕ endure
   - Ⓖ happily
   - Ⓗ rugged
   - Ⓙ weariness

3. He will race against two _____.
   - Ⓐ friend
   - Ⓑ hardy
   - Ⓒ trains
   - Ⓓ opponents

4. Her _____ will not let her quit.
   - Ⓕ shoes
   - Ⓖ mother's
   - Ⓗ determination
   - Ⓙ overcome

5. A runner must be _____.
   - Ⓐ grow
   - Ⓑ strongly
   - Ⓒ opponents
   - Ⓓ hardy

6. A runner cannot give in to _____.
   - Ⓕ weariness
   - Ⓖ goal
   - Ⓗ late
   - Ⓙ lonely

7. Pain can be hard to _____.
   - Ⓐ color
   - Ⓑ endure
   - Ⓒ smile
   - Ⓓ loneliness

8. She must _____ her fear of animals to have a pet.
   - Ⓕ victory
   - Ⓖ rabbit
   - Ⓗ overcome
   - Ⓙ welcome

9. _____ makes her wish for company.
   - Ⓐ Loneliness
   - Ⓑ Apples
   - Ⓒ Difficult
   - Ⓓ Waited

10. A _____ makes a team happy!
    - Ⓕ victory
    - Ⓖ rugged
    - Ⓗ defeat
    - Ⓙ conquer

Review

1. A runner who wins a race is _____.
   - Ⓐ happily
   - Ⓑ delayed
   - Ⓒ triumphant
   - Ⓓ better

2. A man-made moon is called a _____.
   - Ⓕ sun
   - Ⓖ data
   - Ⓗ starry
   - Ⓙ satellite

The Tarahumara run together as a team. They help each other to achieve their goal of victory.

On the lines below, write about a time when you were part of a team. A team could be you and a friend, a group of friends, or even your family. How did you work together? What was your goal? Use some vocabulary words in your writing.

Turn to "My Word List" on page 132. Write some words from the story or other words that you would like to know more about. Use a dictionary to find the meanings.

_____

_____

_____

_____

_____

_____

_____

_____

_____

_____

_____

★ To review the words in Lessons 9–12, turn to page 127. ★

MOUNTAINS' MYSTERIES

Mountains are wonders of nature. Many people enjoy the magnificent beauty of mountains. Others see a mountain and know they have to climb it.

In Lessons 13 - 16, you will read about the wonders and mysteries of mountains. Imagine that you have climbed to the top of a very high mountain. What words describe the mountain? What words describe your feelings? Write your words under the headings below.

The Mountain	My Feelings
_____	_____
_____	_____
_____	_____
_____	_____

★ Read the story below. Think about the meanings of the **boldfaced** words. ★

Climbing Mount Everest

Edmund Hillary and Tenzing Norgay push their way through the snow. They look like visitors from another planet. They wear heavy suits, hoods, and goggles. They are tied together by a 12-foot rope. The date is May 29, 1953. The two men are **ascending** Mount Everest. It is the highest mountain in the world. They hope to reach its peak today.

Mount Everest is part of the Himalaya mountain range north of India. It rises 5-1/2 miles above sea level. Near the top of the mountain, the air is thin, and breathing is hard. Temperatures drop far below freezing. The wind is fierce. Mt. Everest is a **treacherous** mountain.

Before Hillary and Norgay, seven climbing teams had tried to reach the top of Mount Everest. All of them had failed. Sixteen men had died trying to reach the **mountaintop**.

Hillary, from New Zealand, and Norgay, from Nepal, climb **uphill** slowly. They creep along at about 250 feet an hour. The last 1,100 feet are the worst. They move inch by inch up a dangerous **crest**. It crumbles under their feet. The air is so thin, they must breathe through **oxygen masks**.

The final 500-foot climb to the top is very icy. With **heroic** effort, the two men push on. As they go, they cut steps in the snow. At 11:30 A.M., they reach the top. It is a **breathtaking** view! Most people could not even imagine this sight. The two men celebrate their **arrival** by shaking hands. Below them lie the ridges and peaks of the Himalayas. Edmund Hillary and Tenzing Norgay have made history. It has been an **incredible** day.

★ Go back to the story. Underline the words or sentences that give you a clue to the meaning of each **boldfaced** word. ★

CONTEXT CLUES

Read each sentence below. Choose a word from the box that means the same as the underlined part of each sentence. Write the word on the line after the sentence.

incredible	arrival	crest	breathtaking
treacherous	heroic	oxygen masks	ascending
mountaintop	uphill		

1. It takes <u>extremely brave</u> people to try to climb Mount Everest. _____

2. Such a climb is <u>very dangerous</u>. _____

3. They are climbing <u>up the slope of a hill</u>. _____

4. Up that high, they breathe through <u>equipment that supplies the gas that all living things need</u>. _____

5. The climbers keep on <u>going up</u> anyway. _____

6. They must reach the <u>mountain's peak</u>. _____

7. The climb can offer sights that are so beautiful they are <u>hard to believe</u>. _____

8. Climbers know they are near the end of the climb when they reach <u>the top part</u> of the mountain. _____

9. Their <u>reaching of the journey's end</u> at the top means they are at the highest tip of the world. _____

10. It is a <u>thrilling and exciting</u> view from the top of Mount Everest. _____

SYNONYMS

Synonyms are words that have the same or almost the same meaning. Match the words in the box with their synonyms listed below. Write each word on the line.

mountaintop	heroic	treacherous	incredible

1. peak _____

2. unbelievable _____

3. dangerous _____

4. fearless _____

MULTIPLE MEANINGS

The words in the box have more than one meaning. Look for clues in each sentence to tell which meaning is being used. Write the letter of the meaning next to the correct sentence.

crest	uphill	arrival
a. the top part	**a.** toward a higher place	**a.** the reaching of the journey's end
b. feathers on the head of a bird	**b.** difficult	**b.** person who arrives

_____ **1.** A jungle bird will often have a <u>crest</u>.

_____ **2.** They were riding in on the <u>crest</u> of the wave.

_____ **3.** The plane's <u>arrival</u> has been announced.

_____ **4.** She is a new <u>arrival</u> from another country.

_____ **5.** The trail is all <u>uphill</u>.

_____ **6.** It will be an <u>uphill</u> fight to win the race.

HIDDEN MESSAGE PUZZLE

Write a word from the box next to each clue. To find the message, copy the numbered letters in the matching numbered boxes at the bottom of the page. Then you will know where all mountain climbers want to go.

treacherous	incredible	crest	heroic	oxygen masks
breathtaking	ascending	uphill	arrival	mountaintop

1. going up

2. thrilling
b r e a t h t a k i n g
(4 under 4th box)

3. brave and bold
H E R O I C
(2 under 4th box)

4. the top part
C R E S T
(1 under 5th box)

5. peak of a mountain
m o u n t a i n t o p
(3)

6. a climber's direction
u p h i l l
(8 under 2nd box)

7. very dangerous
t r e a h a r o u s
(6 under 1st box)

8. used for breathing
O X Y _ _ _ _ _ _ _ S
(7 under 1st box)

9. the coming to a place
A R R I V A L

10. impossible to believe
i n c r e d i b l e
(5)

ANSWER:
T [ ] - [ ][ ][ ]- T O P !
1 2   3 4 5   6 7 8

Directions: Fill in the space for the word that has the same or almost the same meaning as the boldfaced word.

Always read all the answer choices. Many choices may make sense. But only one answer choice has the same or almost the same meaning as the **boldfaced** word.

1. **treacherous** slope
   - (A) safe
   - (B) pretty
   - (C) dangerous
   - (D) thrilling

2. reach the **mountaintop**
   - (F) peak
   - (G) bottom
   - (H) trees
   - (J) movement

3. climbing **uphill**
   - (A) downward
   - (B) better
   - (C) faster
   - (D) higher

4. wave's **crest**
   - (F) water
   - (G) top
   - (H) inside
   - (J) middle

5. **incredible** view
   - (A) intelligent
   - (B) unbelievable
   - (C) sad
   - (D) bad

6. **ascending** the hill
   - (F) going up
   - (G) going to
   - (H) asking
   - (J) buying

7. **heroic** effort
   - (A) weak
   - (B) heavy
   - (C) little
   - (D) brave

8. **arrival** time
   - (F) leaving
   - (G) coming
   - (H) wanting
   - (J) waiting

9. use **oxygen masks**
   - (A) breathing equipment
   - (B) costumes
   - (C) guns
   - (D) cups

10. **breathtaking** moment
   - (F) long
   - (G) short
   - (H) breathing
   - (J) thrilling

Review

1. important **victory**
   - (A) defeat
   - (B) success
   - (C) vote
   - (D) person

2. **rugged** trail
   - (F) rough
   - (G) rubber
   - (H) smooth
   - (J) indoor

3. **overcome** fear
   - (A) go by
   - (B) outrun
   - (C) conquer
   - (D) have

4. **hardy** animal
   - (F) weak
   - (G) happy
   - (H) stupid
   - (J) strong

Writing

It takes bravery to climb a mountain. It also takes bravery to do many everyday jobs, like being a fire fighter or a police officer.

On the lines below, describe a brave person you know about. The person may be a child or an adult. He or she may be someone you have met or a character on television or in a movie. Explain what the person does that makes him or her brave. Use some vocabulary words in your writing.

My idea of a brave person is _____

_____

_____

_____

_____

_____

_____

_____

_____

_____

_____

_____

_____

Turn to "My Word List" on page 132. Write some words from the story or other words that you would like to know more about. Use a dictionary to find the meanings.

★ Read the story below. Think about the meanings of the **boldfaced** words. ★

Mountain Mist

Lost on her beloved mountain in Scotland, Meg becomes frightened as she remembers a tale her grandmother told her.

Tears welled up in Meg MacRae's eyes as she looked around her. Where were the trails and landmarks she knew so well? Only minutes before, her beloved mountain, High Crag, had been bathed in sunlight and Meg felt at home. Now the sun was **blotted** out by a low cloud. Almost immediately, the crag seemed dark and alien.

As the mist thickened and swirled around her, Meg wished very much that she had listened to her mother. Mrs. MacRae had warned her not to come up on High Crag today.

"Hear me well, lassie," her mother had said. "The Crag will be **smothered** in fog and mist afore this day is through. Should ye climb there today, ye may not see to come back down."

Meg hadn't listened, and now her mother's words had come true. Worse than that, though, was an old Scottish tale that kept repeating itself in Meg's mind. Long ago her grandmother used to tell her stories of spirits and ghosts. One especially frightened the young girl.

> *When the mist has covered all,*
> *And everything looks gray,*
> *'Tis when the Kelpies come to*
>   *call*
> *And spirit you away.*

"I'm not a wee lass anymore!" she said aloud to give herself courage. "Kelpies are only fairy tales!"

With a shake of her dark red braids, she started in what seemed to be the direction of home. Kelpies were said to be **evil** water spirits that had the shape of ponies. They would **graze** on the banks of rivers and **lochs**. When someone drowned, it was said a Kelpie had carried him away.

Finally Meg reached level ground, but the mist was still there. It was so thick she could barely see the heather on which she walked.

"I can't be far from home now." A loud splash came from the loch. Meg jumped. Then she laughed at herself. A fish must have leaped from the water to catch a tasty bug. As another sound came to her ears, Meg grew pale. Clearly through the fog, there came the sound of hoofbeats. Meg panicked. Trying to stay by the edge of the loch, she ran **desperately** away from the sound.

"Meg MacRae, Meg MacRae!" The voice sounded strange and **haunting** to Meg's frightened ears. The voice rang out again, calling her name. It began to sound familiar. She stopped altogether and tried to call out, but her voice **issued** only a quiet squeak. Clearing her throat, she tried again.

"Who is calling for Meg MacRae?" she shouted into the mist.

"Where are ye, lass?" the voice boomed. "'Tis only I, Roy Dougal. Your mother's fair worried and sent me to look."

"Roy," Meg called in relief, "I'm here, by the loch."

"Stay put, lass," Roy called. "Keep speaking, and I'll find you in a twinkling."

The hoofbeats neared, and soon Roy appeared almost magically from the mist. He was **astride** his roan **stallion**.

"Oh, Roy!" she cried. "When I heard the horse, I thought you were a Kelpie coming to get me."

"A Kelpie now, is it?" Roy exclaimed. "Don't tell me a lass such as you believes in fairy tales!"

"No, I don't. Not really," said Meg. "But everyone is afraid sometimes."

From <u>Mountain Mist</u>,
by Pam Sandlin

★ Go back to the story. Underline any words or sentences that give you clues to the meanings of the **boldfaced** words. ★

USING CONTEXT

Meanings for the vocabulary words are given below. Go back to the story and read each sentence that has a vocabulary word. If you still cannot tell the meaning, look for clues in the sentences that come before and after the one with the vocabulary word. Write each word in front of its meaning.

smothered	graze	stallion	desperately
haunting	evil	blotted	astride
issued	lochs		

1. _____: gave; sent out

2. _____: seated with one leg on each side of something

3. _____: to feed on grass

4. _____: blanketed; covered thickly

5. _____: anxiously

6. _____: lakes in Scotland

7. _____: a male horse

8. _____: covered up entirely; hidden

9. _____: wicked; very bad

10. _____: spooky; frightening

CHALLENGE YOURSELF

Name two animals that graze.

_____   _____

Name something that is issued daily.

_____

ANALOGIES

An **analogy** shows how two words go together in the same way as two other words. Write the words from the box to complete the following analogies.

loch	evil	graze	stallion	haunt

1. Drink is to water as _____ is to grass.

2. Prowl is to cat as _____ is to ghost.

3. Mean is to nice as _____ is to good.

4. Bull is to cow as _____ is to mare.

5. Lassie is to girl as _____ is to lake.

DICTIONARY SKILLS

Turn to page 133 in the Dictionary. Use the **pronunciation key** to help you learn how to say the vocabulary words in ( ) in the sentences below. Write the regular spelling for each word in ( ).

1. The man (ish′ üd) a warning. _____

2. We looked (des′pər it lē) for her. _____

3. The cloud (blot′ id) out the sun. _____

4. The cake was (smu<u>th</u>′ərd) in sauce. _____

5. He sat (ə strīd′) the fence. _____

6. A thick mist covered the (lok). _____

7. The (stal′yən) is my fastest horse. _____

8. The cows (grāz) in the field. _____

9. An (ē′vəl) character scared me. _____

GET WISE TO TESTS

Directions: Fill in the space for the word that fits best in the sentence.

 Be sure to mark the answer space correctly. Do <u>not</u> mark the circle with an X or with a checkmark (✓). Instead, fill in the circle neatly and completely with your pencil.

1. The warning was sent out. It was _____.
   - Ⓐ tired
   - Ⓑ issued
   - Ⓒ haunted
   - Ⓓ broken

2. The male horse is beautiful. It is a black _____.
   - Ⓕ stallion
   - Ⓖ mare
   - Ⓗ loch
   - Ⓙ calf

3. The cows will eat in this field. They will _____ here.
   - Ⓐ laugh
   - Ⓑ smother
   - Ⓒ graze
   - Ⓓ order

4. He tried anxiously to reach her. He was _____ concerned.
   - Ⓕ happily
   - Ⓖ carefully
   - Ⓗ hardly
   - Ⓙ desperately

5. We were completely covered by a pile of leaves. We were _____.
   - Ⓐ smothered
   - Ⓑ standing
   - Ⓒ grazed
   - Ⓓ opened

6. There are many lakes in Scotland. In that country, they are called _____.
   - Ⓕ rivers
   - Ⓖ oceans
   - Ⓗ lochs
   - Ⓙ stallions

7. She sat with one leg on each side of the horse. She was _____ it.
   - Ⓐ astride
   - Ⓑ haunting
   - Ⓒ carrying
   - Ⓓ aboard

8. The music was frightening. It sounded _____.
   - Ⓕ cheerful
   - Ⓖ smothering
   - Ⓗ haunting
   - Ⓙ calming

9. The witch in the story was wicked. She did _____ things.
   - Ⓐ kind
   - Ⓑ evil
   - Ⓒ funny
   - Ⓓ wonderful

10. You could not see the sun. The clouds _____ it out.
    - Ⓕ painted
    - Ⓖ issued
    - Ⓗ chased
    - Ⓙ blotted

Writing

In the story, Meg does not pay attention to her mother's warning. She goes for a walk on the mountain and gets lost in the fog. She has to be rescued by a neighbor. Think about a time when you or someone you know did not pay attention to a warning.

On the lines below, tell about the warning and why it wasn't obeyed. What happened? Use some vocabulary words in your writing.

Turn to "My Word List" on page 132. Write some words from the story or other words you would like to know more about. Use a dictionary to find the meanings.

★ Read the story below. Think about the meanings of the **boldfaced** words. ★

A Wonder of Nature

The Rocky Mountains are one of nature's wonders. They are the largest mountain range in North America. They **extend** more than 3,000 miles through the western United States and Canada.

Visitors to the Rockies marvel at the spectacular mountains. If they look **upward**, they see snowcapped peaks. If they look downward from above, they see dark **gorges**. These deep, narrow openings between the sides of the mountains look as if they go on forever. If visitors were to explore the inside of these mountains, they would find huge **caverns**. These caves were formed millions of years ago along with the peaks and gorges.

How were the Rocky Mountains formed? What was their **origin**? **Geologists** who study the earth's makeup explain that the earth is always in a state of change. Inside the earth, below the top layer called the **crust**, there are layers of rock. At one time, deep inside those layers it was very hot. The rock became so hot that it was **heaved** above the crust and into the air. When the hot rock flowed down, it **deposited** high piles in some places and cut deep openings in others. When it cooled, the Rocky Mountains had been born.

Over millions of years, the forces in nature — wind, rain, and ice — shaped the mountains. This shaping made parts of the mountains smoother and rounder and other parts sharper with steep cliffs. Parts of mountains even **collapsed**, or fell in, creating bowl-shaped holes.

Whether on the ground or in the air, all who have seen the Rocky Mountains agree. They are a true wonder of nature.

★ Go back to the story. Underline the words or sentences that give you a clue to the meaning of each **boldfaced** word. ★

CONTEXT CLUES

In each sentence, one word is underlined. That word sounds silly in the sentence. Choose a word from the box that can replace the word that sounds silly. Write it on the line.

heaved	collapsed	gorges	geologists
caverns	deposited	crust	extend
origin	upward		

1. <u>Dancers</u> study mountains. _geologists_

2. They look for the <u>peak</u>, or beginning. _origin_

3. They know that molten rock was thrown, or <u>skated</u>, out from inside the earth. _heaved_

4. The rock came up through the <u>peel</u>, the top layer of the earth. _crust_

5. The rock that was <u>measured</u>, or left, on the earth's surface formed the Rocky Mountains. _deposited_

6. Deep openings, or <u>doors</u>, were formed. _gorges_

7. Caves, or <u>toys</u>, were also formed. _caverns_

8. Bowl-shaped holes were created when sections of the mountain range fell in, or <u>crawled</u>. _collapsed_

9. The mountains seem to climb <u>slowly</u>, or toward a higher place, for miles. _upward_

10. The Rocky Mountains stretch out, or <u>shrink</u>, so far they cover several states! _extend_

WORD GROUPS

Read each pair of words. Think about how they are alike. Write the word from the box that best completes each group.

geologist	cavern	heaved	gorge	crust
origin	upward			

1. beginning, source, _____

2. hurled, threw, _____

3. teacher, astronaut, _____

4. uphill, uptown, _____

5. skin, bark, _____

6. cave, den, _____

7. canyon, valley, _____

WRITING SENTENCES

Use each vocabulary word in the box to write an original sentence.

gorge	deposit	extend	collapse	cavern
origin	geologist			

1. _____

2. _____

3. _____

4. _____

5. _____

6. _____

7. _____

Directions: Read each sentence carefully. Then choose the best answer to complete each sentence. Mark the space for the answer you have chosen.

 Read carefully. Use the other words in the sentence to help you choose the missing word.

1. **Gorges** are deep openings in _____.
   Ⓐ leaves   © mountains
   Ⓑ oceans   Ⓓ clouds

2. A **geologist** studies the _____.
   Ⓕ stars   Ⓗ children
   Ⓖ earth   Ⓙ animals

3. When the house **collapsed**, it _____.
   Ⓐ fell in   © came out
   Ⓑ raised up   Ⓓ went up

4. When a ball is **heaved**, it is _____ hard.
   Ⓕ sat on   Ⓗ made
   Ⓖ caught   Ⓙ thrown

5. When you go **upward**, you are going to a _____ place.
   Ⓐ lower   © darker
   Ⓑ higher   Ⓓ shorter

6. The **crust** is the top layer of the _____.
   Ⓕ ocean   Ⓗ earth
   Ⓖ clouds   Ⓙ air

7. The **origin** of something is its _____.
   Ⓐ beginning   © death
   Ⓑ color   Ⓓ surface

8. Another name for **caverns** is _____.
   Ⓕ candles   Ⓗ bats
   Ⓖ windows   Ⓙ caves

9. Dirt **deposited** by a storm is _____ by it.
   Ⓐ left   © cut
   Ⓑ welcomed   Ⓓ upside-down

10. When stores **extend** a sale, the sale is _____.
   Ⓕ over   Ⓗ stretched out
   Ⓖ started   Ⓙ burned out

Review

1. A **haunting** story is _____.
   Ⓐ funny   © happy
   Ⓑ scary   Ⓓ boring

2. When horses **graze**, they _____.
   Ⓕ sleep   Ⓗ play
   Ⓖ fight   Ⓙ eat

Pretend that your family is planning a vacation. Some members want to go to the seashore. You want to visit the Rocky Mountains.

On the lines below, write what you would say to your family to convince everyone to go to the mountains. Give your reasons for choosing the mountains over the seashore. Use the picture to help you with details. Use some vocabulary words in your writing.

I think we should go to the mountains instead of the seashore

because _____

_____

_____

_____

_____

_____

_____

_____

_____

_____

_____

_____

_____

Turn to "My Word List" on page 132. Write some words from the story or other words that you would like to know more about. Use a dictionary to find the meanings.

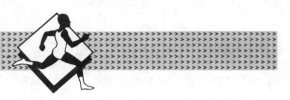
★ Read the story below. Think about the meanings of
the **boldfaced** words. ★

A "Peak" Experience

A climber might be a **beginner**. She might be an expert. Either way, there is a school that will help this young person **achieve** her outdoor goals. Outward Bound offers training for many outdoor adventures, including mountain climbing. Young people might have bodies that are in really good shape, or they might not. Whether or not they have great **physical** abilities, they can learn to climb mountains.

Mountain-climbing students, in small groups, take a course that can last about three weeks. The students learn to read maps. They learn safety rules to help them **avoid** careless accidents. They pay close attention to the directions. They **concentrate** on each thing they need to learn. For example, they spend time learning the proper use of their **gear**, the equipment they need for a climb.

The students look up to their Outward Bound teachers. Each teacher is an **inspiration** to the young people. The teachers make the young people want to meet difficult challenges. They guide the students through climbing skills. They help students learn how to make choices. And they help them learn to work together.

The group works together to plan a mountain-climbing trip. When the climb is finished, the students have done something important for themselves. Everyone respects what the group has **accomplished**. Each member earns and **deserves** the praise and cheers of the teachers and other students.

Most people want to prove themselves. They have a **desire** to succeed. Outward Bound helps many young people do just that. They believe that a person who climbs a mountain can reach other peaks in life, too.

★ Go back to the story. Underline the words or sentences that give
you a clue to the meaning of each **boldfaced** word. ★

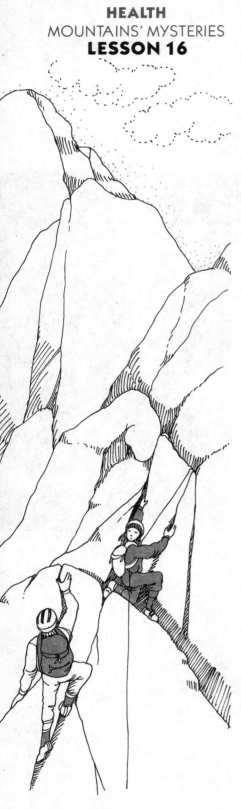

USING CONTEXT

Meanings for the vocabulary words are given below. Go back to the story and read each sentence that has a vocabulary word. If you still cannot tell the meaning, look for clues in the sentences that come before and after the one with the vocabulary word. Write each word in front of its meaning.

concentrate	gear	achieve	avoid
accomplished	desire	inspiration	deserves
beginner	physical		

1. _____ : having to do with the body

2. _____ : someone just starting to learn something

3. _____ : to keep away from

4. _____ : equipment used for a particular purpose

5. _____ : to pay very close attention

6. _____ : a longing; a strong wish

7. _____ : a person that other people look up to

8. _____ : carried out; done

9. _____ : has a right to; is worthy of

10. _____ : to succeed in reaching a goal

CHALLENGE YOURSELF

Name two pieces of <u>gear</u> you would take on a fishing trip.

_____   _____

Name two activities in which you are a <u>beginner</u>.

_____   _____

MULTIPLE MEANINGS

The words in the box have more than one meaning. Look for clues in each sentence to tell which meaning is being used. Write the letter of the meaning next to the correct sentence.

gear	concentrate	physical
a. equipment	**a.** pay close attention	**a.** relating to the body
b. machine part	**b.** to bring close together in one place	**b.** a medical checkup

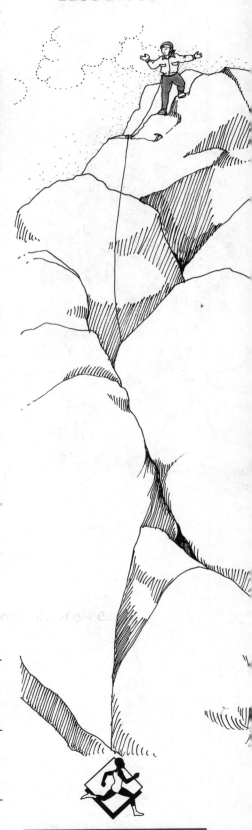

_____ **1.** The airplane pilot put down the landing <u>gear</u>.

_____ **2.** Pack the camping <u>gear</u> in the trunk of the car.

_____ **3.** Sue must <u>concentrate</u> on finishing her homework.

_____ **4.** The workers will all <u>concentrate</u> in the dining room.

_____ **5.** The doctor will give her a complete <u>physical</u>.

_____ **6.** Swimming is good <u>physical</u> exercise.

REWRITING SENTENCES

Rewrite each sentence using one of the vocabulary words from the box.

avoid	desire	deserves

1. My brother is worthy of a medal for putting up with me!

_____

2. My dad said that we should keep away from poison ivy.

_____

3. To be a champion, you need the strong wish to win.

_____

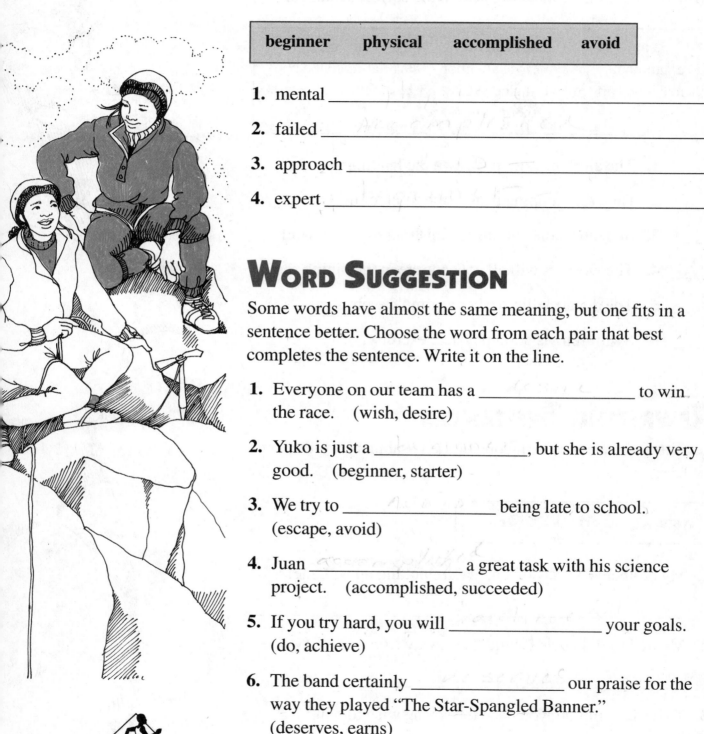

ANTONYMS

Remember that **antonyms** are words that have opposite meanings. Match the words in the box with their antonyms listed below. Write each word on the line.

beginner	physical	accomplished	avoid

1. mental _____

2. failed _____

3. approach _____

4. expert _____

WORD SUGGESTION

Some words have almost the same meaning, but one fits in a sentence better. Choose the word from each pair that best completes the sentence. Write it on the line.

1. Everyone on our team has a _____ to win the race.   (wish, desire)

2. Yuko is just a _____, but she is already very good.   (beginner, starter)

3. We try to _____ being late to school. (escape, avoid)

4. Juan _____ a great task with his science project.   (accomplished, succeeded)

5. If you try hard, you will _____ your goals. (do, achieve)

6. The band certainly _____ our praise for the way they played "The Star-Spangled Banner." (deserves, earns)

Directions: Find the word that means the same, or about the same, as the boldfaced word. Mark your answer.

This test will show how well you understand the meaning of the words. Think about the meaning of the **boldfaced** word before you choose your answer.

1. **concentrate** on work
   - Ⓐ rest your head
   - Ⓑ set your mind
   - Ⓒ set your clock
   - Ⓓ turn around

2. **achieve** a goal
   - Ⓕ set
   - Ⓖ reach
   - Ⓗ fail
   - Ⓙ forget

3. camping **gear**
   - Ⓐ trails
   - Ⓑ days
   - Ⓒ equipment
   - Ⓓ jokes

4. **physical** shape
   - Ⓕ mind
   - Ⓖ body
   - Ⓗ feelings
   - Ⓙ country

5. just a **beginner**
   - Ⓐ new learner
   - Ⓑ expert
   - Ⓒ manager
   - Ⓓ diver

6. **deserves** praise
   - Ⓕ needs
   - Ⓖ gives
   - Ⓗ wants
   - Ⓙ earns

7. **accomplished** much
   - Ⓐ has done
   - Ⓑ has cried
   - Ⓒ has played
   - Ⓓ has spent

8. **inspiration** to many
   - Ⓕ source of laughter
   - Ⓖ source of light
   - Ⓗ source of encouragement
   - Ⓙ source of trouble

9. **avoid** problems
   - Ⓐ rush toward
   - Ⓑ tell about
   - Ⓒ do
   - Ⓓ keep away from

10. a strong **desire**
    - Ⓕ wish
    - Ⓖ spice
    - Ⓗ rope
    - Ⓙ smell

Review

1. dark **caverns**
   - Ⓐ oceans
   - Ⓑ caves
   - Ⓒ roads
   - Ⓓ hills

2. mountain's **origin**
   - Ⓕ color
   - Ⓖ size
   - Ⓗ name
   - Ⓙ beginning

3. **collapsed** suddenly
   - Ⓐ fell in
   - Ⓑ sat down
   - Ⓒ drowned
   - Ⓓ raised up

4. Earth's **crust**
   - Ⓕ grass
   - Ⓖ bottom layer
   - Ⓗ pie
   - Ⓙ top layer

5. **extend** the visit
   - Ⓐ welcome
   - Ⓑ stretch out
   - Ⓒ bring out
   - Ⓓ shorten

Writing

The Outward Bound students who want to climb mountains achieve their goal. You could say that they have fulfilled a desire. What is something that you desire to do with your life?

On the lines below, tell about a goal that you would like to achieve. Why is this goal important to you? What can you do to help you fulfill your desire? Use some vocabulary words in your writing.

_____

_____

_____

_____

_____

_____

_____

_____

_____

_____

_____

_____

_____

_____

_____

_____

Turn to "My Word List" on page 132. Write some words from the story or other words that you would like to know more about. Use a dictionary to find the meanings.

★ To review the words in Lessons 13–16, turn to page 128. ★

ON STAGE

We see some shows that are live. We see others on a screen. Either way, these shows are meant to entertain us.

In Lessons 17 - 20, you will read about different kinds of shows. Think about the shows you like. What do you like about each one? Do you like the characters or the story? Do you like the costumes or the music? Write some words that tell about the shows you like on the lines below.

Movies and Television	Live Concerts
_____	_____
_____	_____
_____	_____
_____	_____
_____	_____

★ Read the story below. Think about the meanings of the **boldfaced** words. ★

Big Screen, Little Screen

"Ready for **broadcast**. 5 − 4 − 3 − 2 − 1! We're on the air!" The next second, television programs are brought into people's homes. This happens by sending **communication** signals through the air.

Work on televisions began in the early 1900s. But it was 1936 before people could buy them. The first show people saw on television was a cartoon.

Television started to take hold in the early 1950s. The major **networks** were in New York City. These large stations were connected to smaller stations across the country. People watched news and sports shows. Other shows were made just for people's **pleasure**. People enjoyed watching them. Many things were **advertised** for people to buy just as they are today.

Some shows were live. Others were on film. I Love Lucy was one popular show on film. It began in 1951. What made the show such a hit was Lucy. The **situations** she found herself in were like what happened to people every day. The way Lucy handled them was funny, silly, even **ridiculous**! Yet everything always worked out. Maybe that is why **generations** of people have watched the show over the years.

Beginning in the 1960s, television was not only entertaining. Viewers could also watch **educational** shows. People could learn about the world by watching television.

Big screen or little screen, it doesn't matter. Just push a button to get a different **channel**. Who knows what you will see next!

★ Go back to the story. Underline the words or sentences that give you a clue to the meaning of each **boldfaced** word. ★

CONTEXT CLUES

Read each sentence. Look for clues to help you complete
each sentence with a word from the box. Write the word
on the line.

broadcast	**generations**	**channel**	**advertised**
pleasure	**communication**	**educational**	**networks**
situations	**ridiculous**		

1. Most cities have their own television stations. These

   stations form large television _____ across
   the country.

2. Every _____ tells you something.

3. You could say that every program is a form of

   _____.

4. One station has the _____ programs that teach.

5. I often push the button on my remote control for this

   _____.

6. Many people enjoy watching movies or sports on television.

   These shows give them a lot of _____.

7. Others like funny shows where the people act silly. They

   laugh when the characters do _____ things
   on these programs.

8. Sometimes television shows remind you of events in your

   own life. The _____ may be very familiar.

9. Some people do not like the commercials on television. They

   leave the room when products are _____.

10. Television has changed since my grandmother first watched

    it. What will it be like for future _____?

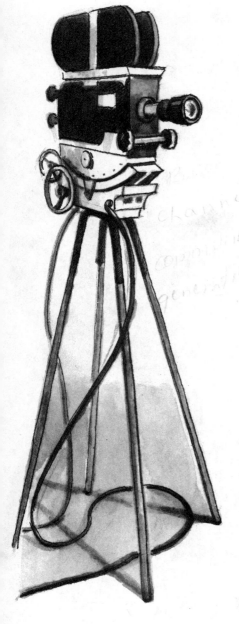

DICTIONARY SKILLS

Remember that **guide words** are the two words at the top of each dictionary page. They show the first and last entries on that page. All the word entries are in alphabetical order. Look at the pairs of guide words. On the lines below each pair, write the words from the box that would appear on the same dictionary page. Be sure to put them in alphabetical order.

channel	situation	broadcast
pleasure	ridiculous	generation
networks	communication	

baby / giant

1. _____
2. _____
3. _____
4. _____

nest / strike

5. _____
6. _____
7. _____
8. _____

BASE WORDS

Remember that **base words** are words without any endings or other word parts added to them. For each vocabulary word below, write its base word next to it on the line. Sometimes the spelling of the base word changes when an ending is added to it. Turn to the Dictionary, beginning on page 133, if you need help spelling the base words.

1. networks _____

2. communication _____

3. advertised _____

4. educational _____

WORD MAP

Use the vocabulary words in the box to complete the word map about television. Add other words that you know to each group.

pleasure	educational	ridiculous	broadcasts
situations	advertises		

What You See

1. _____
2. _____
3. _____
4. _____

Kinds of Programs

1. _____
2. _____
3. _____
4. _____

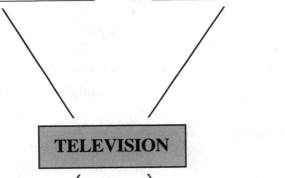

TELEVISION

What It Gives

1. _____
2. _____
3. _____
4. _____

What It Does

1. _____
2. _____
3. _____
4. _____

GET WISE TO TESTS

Directions: Read each sentence. Pick the word that best completes the sentence. Mark the letter for that word.

 Tip If you are not sure which word completes the sentence, do the best you can. Try to choose the answer that makes the most sense.

1. _____ have many stations.
   Ⓐ Networks   Ⓒ Ridiculous
   Ⓑ Situations   Ⓓ Fires

2. Some _____ are not funny.
   Ⓕ clowning   Ⓗ situations
   Ⓖ advertised   Ⓙ monkey

3. _____ has been difficult, so we have not talked.
   Ⓐ Count   Ⓒ Generations
   Ⓑ Speaks   Ⓓ Communication

4. Is this show ready for a _____?
   Ⓕ channels   Ⓗ ridiculous
   Ⓖ viewed   Ⓙ broadcast

5. My mother and I are from different _____.
   Ⓐ planets   Ⓒ moved
   Ⓑ generations   Ⓓ time

6. My pet gives me a lot of _____.
   Ⓕ troubling   Ⓗ pleasure
   Ⓖ bone   Ⓙ money

7. I saw that toy _____ on television.
   Ⓐ broke   Ⓒ make
   Ⓑ playful   Ⓓ advertised

8. I learn a lot from the _____ programs.
   Ⓕ educational   Ⓗ sported
   Ⓖ bake   Ⓙ child

9. Which _____ do you watch the most?
   Ⓐ advertised   Ⓒ sound
   Ⓑ channel   Ⓓ communication

10. That silly show is _____.
    Ⓕ laughing   Ⓗ seriously
    Ⓖ sad   Ⓙ ridiculous

Writing

Think about an idea for an interesting television program for students.

Write to the head of a television network and describe your idea. Give two reasons why the network should produce the show. Use some vocabulary words in your writing.

_____

(Date)

Dear _____:

I like many of the shows on your network. But I have an idea

for a new one. I think students would watch a show about _____

_____

_____

_____

_____

_____

_____

_____

_____

_____

_____

Sincerely yours,

_____

Turn to "My Word List" on page 132. Write some words from the story or other words you would like to know more about. Use a dictionary to find the meanings.

★ Read the story below. Think about the meanings of the **boldfaced** words. ★

Popcorn

Mark Newman has big plans for his group, Popcorn. He thinks he and his friends, Missy and Richard, have the talent to make it to the top of the music world. Mark tells about a letter that just may get them on stage.

After I finished my homework that night I sat on my bed reading the music magazine that had come in the mail that day. I started to doze off, but when I actually fell asleep and rolled over, a crinkling sound woke me up. It was the junk mail Ma had said she'd left on my bed. I picked it up. The return address on the envelope was Porcupine Records Corporation. Wilshire Boulevard! Los Angeles, California! I couldn't believe that Ma would call such an incredible thing "junk mail." My heart started thumping. My eyes flew open. Suddenly I was wide awake again and my hands were trembling. I tore open the envelope and pulled out the letter. It said:

Dear Songwriter:

   The **major** recording companies must continue to find and record fresh new songs. The strength of the music industry is in your hands, and that is why we are writing to you. We **urge** you to let us look over your work so that we might give you an **honest opinion**. If we decide to record your song on a commercial recording **agreement**, we will ship records to **disc jockeys** and record stores and pay you a share for each record sold. This could make you a star.

   Please send us no more than three (3) of your best songs on cassette, with an **accompanying** lyric sheet for each song. As soon as we receive your material we will **review** it and you will have our opinion as quickly as possible.

Thank you. I look forward to hearing from you.

Musically yours,

William S. Shartner

Recording **Director**

**From Popcorn, by Gary Provost
and Gail Levine-Provost**

My hands were still shaking when I finished reading the letter. I read it again. How did they find out about me? I wondered. I knew this could be Popcorn's big break. I wanted to call Richard and Missy, but it was too late. I ran to the closet and lugged out my big box of cassettes. I pulled out a tape I had just made. On it were my two best songs, "Pop Some Corn," which is Popcorn's **theme** song, and "It's Good If It Goes," which is the song I wrote for my brother. I knew that both of them could be million-seller hits.

I typed up the lyric sheets for each song. That took forever because I was using my brother's old typewriter and the keys stick and besides I don't know how to type with more than one finger. Then I put everything in an envelope and addressed it to Porcupine Records. I could smell success. I wished I could run out and mail it right then. I put the package by the door so I'd be sure to mail it before school in the morning. Then I went to bed.

But I couldn't sleep. I tossed back and forth, thinking about what they had written. "The strength of the music industry is in your hands." Strength. Music industry. My hands. Strength. Music industry. My hands. Strength, music industry, my hands. And finally I fell asleep, thinking that I had found my strength.

★ Go back to the story. Underline any words or sentences that give you clues to the meanings of the **boldfaced** words. ★

USING CONTEXT

Meanings for the vocabulary words are given below. Go back
to the story and read each sentence that has a vocabulary word.
If you still cannot tell the meaning, look for clues in the
sentences that come before and after the one with the
vocabulary word. Write each word in front of its meaning.

agreement	urge	accompanying	honest
director	major	disc jockeys	review
opinion	theme		

1. _____: what a person believes about
something

2. _____: an understanding between two or
more people

3. _____: to look at again

4. _____: full of truth

5. _____: person who manages or guides
others

6. _____: melody used to identify performers
or a show

7. _____: more important

8. _____: people at a radio station who play
records and announce songs

9. _____: strongly encourage

10. _____: going along with

REWRITING SENTENCES

Rewrite each sentence using one of the vocabulary words from the box.

agreement	honest	disc jockey	accompanying

1. My brother was going along with me to school.

   _____

2. Our written understanding was signed today.

   _____

3. I like the guy who announces the songs on station WXYZ.

   _____

4. He is a person who does not lie, cheat, or steal.

   _____

SYNONYMS

Synonyms are words that have the same or almost the same meaning. Match the words that are synonyms.

theme	major	review	director
urge	opinion		

1. manager _____

2. belief _____

3. encourage _____

4. melody _____

5. main _____

6. examine _____

GET WISE TO TESTS

Directions: Fill in the space for the word that fits best in the sentence.

 Before you choose an answer, try reading the sentence with each answer choice. This will help you choose an answer that makes sense.

1. She manages the business. She is the _____.
   Ⓐ guest   Ⓒ teacher
   Ⓑ director   Ⓓ theme

2. Mark always tells the truth. He is very _____.
   Ⓕ bad   Ⓗ honest
   Ⓖ friendly   Ⓙ scared

3. That company is more important. It is a _____ airline.
   Ⓐ major   Ⓒ funny
   Ⓑ little   Ⓓ flying

4. They will encourage her to come. I will _____ her also.
   Ⓕ confuse   Ⓗ buy
   Ⓖ review   Ⓙ urge

5. Amy will look over her notes again. She will _____ them for the test.
   Ⓐ mail   Ⓒ review
   Ⓑ burn   Ⓓ urge

6. Tim often asks me what I think. He listens to my _____.
   Ⓕ agreement   Ⓗ stories
   Ⓖ dog   Ⓙ opinion

7. Someone must go along with our team. Who will be _____ us?
   Ⓐ accompanying   Ⓒ urging
   Ⓑ accusing   Ⓓ locating

8. The composer signed the letter of understanding. Now he had an _____.
   Ⓕ director   Ⓗ army
   Ⓖ ache   Ⓙ agreement

9. They play records for a living. They are _____.
   Ⓐ majors   Ⓒ directors
   Ⓑ disc jockeys   Ⓓ composers

10. You always know her by her special melody. It is her _____.
    Ⓕ dress   Ⓗ director
    Ⓖ theme   Ⓙ agreement

Along with the recording of Popcorn's theme song, Mark would have sent a letter. In the letter he would have described the group. Pretend you are Mark. What would you write to Mr. Shartner? How would you convince him to give Popcorn a chance?

Complete the letter below. Use some vocabulary words in your writing.

_____
                    (Date)

Mr. William S. Shartner
Porcupine Records Corporation
Wilshire Boulevard
Los Angeles, California

Dear Mr. Shartner:

The songs on this tape were recorded by Popcorn, my hot

new group. _____

_____

_____

_____

_____

_____

_____

_____

_____

_____

_____

Turn to "My Word List" on page 132. Write some words from the story or other words you would like to know more about. Use a dictionary to find the meanings.

★ Read the story below. Think about the meanings of the **boldfaced** words. ★

Creating the Impossible

People float around rooms. Giant animals attack whole cities. Nails become claws. Faces **dissolve** before your eyes. They change into awful, watery blobs. You know these things cannot really happen. But they are happening in the movies you watch. These make-believe things are called special effects.

The **techniques**, or ways, to make what is not real seem real keep changing. The people who think of the new ideas are the **creators**. They are always trying to come up with better ideas. They want to shock, surprise, and entertain you. Many creators of special effects now use computers to make characters such as monsters and dinosaurs. The computer artist first draws a framework of the character. Then layers of details are added. The result is a dinosaur or monster that looks very real.

Some **processes** for making special effects have been around for years. For example, many effects have been done with very small models. People build the models to **represent**, or stand for, real things. Then they **assemble** them piece by piece. Later, cameras are used to film the models in different ways.

Lighting and sound have long been important in creating special effects. Lights can **flicker** quickly. Lights can **fade** into darkness. Lights can add an air of mystery. **Eerie** music with colored lights can scare you right out of your seat. The creators of special effects are very **imaginative**.

Now we all know that creepy things we see in movies are just special effects. They are not real. And we won't be scared next time we see them, will we?

★ Go back to the story. Underline the words or sentences that give you a clue to the meaning of each **boldfaced** word. ★

USING CONTEXT

Meanings for the vocabulary words are given below. Go back to the story and read each sentence that has a vocabulary word. If you still cannot tell the meaning, look for clues in the sentences that come before and after the one with the vocabulary word. Write each word in front of its meaning.

processes	represent	dissolve	techniques
imaginative	creators	eerie	fade
assemble	flicker		

1. _____fade_____ : to become less bright

2. _____techniques_____ : ways of doing things; methods

3. _____processes_____ : actions done in a special order

4. _____imaginative_____ : able to think of new things easily

5. _____creators_____ : people who design or make things

6. _____assemble_____ : to put or bring together

7. _____dissolve_____ : to become liquid

8. _____flicker_____ : to shine with a light that is not steady; twinkle

9. _____eerie_____ : causing fear; spooky

10. _____represent_____ : to stand for; to be a symbol of

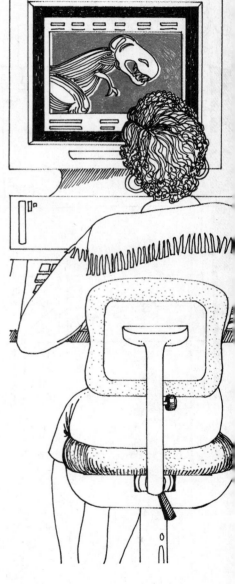

CHALLENGE YOURSELF

Name two things that you think are <u>eerie</u>.

_____cemetery_____ _____

Name two things that <u>dissolve</u>.

_____ _____

SINONIMS.

SYNONYMS

Remember that **synonyms** are words that have the same or almost the same meaning. Cross out the word in each line that is not a synonym.

1. imaginative   creative   (boring)   clever   *inteli gente*
2. fade   *del vanee do* darken   vanish   (glitter)
3. dissolve   melt   disappear   (freeze)
4. assemble   make   (destroy)   (join)
5. eerie   (pretty)   scary   strange

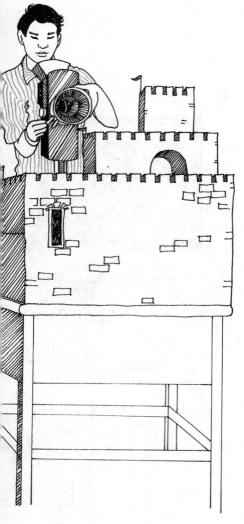

DICTIONARY SKILLS

Turn to page 133 in the Dictionary. Use the **pronunciation** key to help you learn how to say the vocabulary words in ( ) in the sentences below. Write the regular spelling for each word in ( ).

1. What (pros′ es ez) did you use? _____

2. The campfire began to (flik′ ər). _____

3. The (krē ā′ tərz) are clever. _____

4. Does the flag (rep′ ri zent′) freedom? _____

5. The sun will (fād) the tent. _____

6. Watch the ice cube (di zolv′). _____

7. The door made an (îr′ e) sound. _____

8. I enjoy that artist's (tek nēk′). _____

Directions: Find the word that means the same, or almost the same, as the boldfaced word. Mark your answer.

Tip Always read all the answer choices. Many choices may make sense. But only one answer choice has the same or almost the same meaning as the **boldfaced** word.

1. monsters **dissolve**
   - Ⓐ roar
   - Ⓑ destroy
   - Ⓒ melt
   - Ⓓ sleep

2. lights **flicker**
   - Ⓕ sneeze
   - Ⓖ twinkle
   - Ⓗ break
   - Ⓙ come on

3. **imaginative** idea
   - Ⓐ dull
   - Ⓑ made up
   - Ⓒ terrible
   - Ⓓ wrong

4. **eerie** music
   - Ⓕ spooky
   - Ⓖ happy
   - Ⓗ calming
   - Ⓙ funny

5. **represent** me
   - Ⓐ deny
   - Ⓑ stand for
   - Ⓒ stand against
   - Ⓓ report

6. modern **techniques**
   - Ⓕ lights
   - Ⓖ ways
   - Ⓗ people
   - Ⓙ computers

7. talented **creators**
   - Ⓐ inventors
   - Ⓑ films
   - Ⓒ modern
   - Ⓓ crayons

8. special **processes**
   - Ⓕ noises
   - Ⓖ profits
   - Ⓗ methods
   - Ⓙ actors

9. colors **fade**
   - Ⓐ become brighter
   - Ⓑ become better
   - Ⓒ become shorter
   - Ⓓ become less bright

10. **assemble** friends
    - Ⓕ attach
    - Ⓖ destroy
    - Ⓗ gather
    - Ⓙ bother

Review

1. **major** event
   - Ⓐ secret
   - Ⓑ magic
   - Ⓒ important
   - Ⓓ dull

2. good **director**
   - Ⓕ manager
   - Ⓖ enemy
   - Ⓗ friend
   - Ⓙ farmer

3. **urge** her
   - Ⓐ use
   - Ⓑ encourage
   - Ⓒ find
   - Ⓓ forget

4. **accompanying** us
   - Ⓕ enjoying
   - Ⓖ leaving
   - Ⓗ doing without
   - Ⓙ going along with

5. performer's **theme**
   - Ⓐ date
   - Ⓑ show
   - Ⓒ melody
   - Ⓓ jokes

Imagine you are a creator of special effects in movies. You have just been asked to make eerie special effects for a new movie. The star of the movie is your favorite actor or actress.

On the lines below, write about one of the special effects that you will use in the movie. Explain why you think your audience will like this special effect. Use some vocabulary words in your writing.

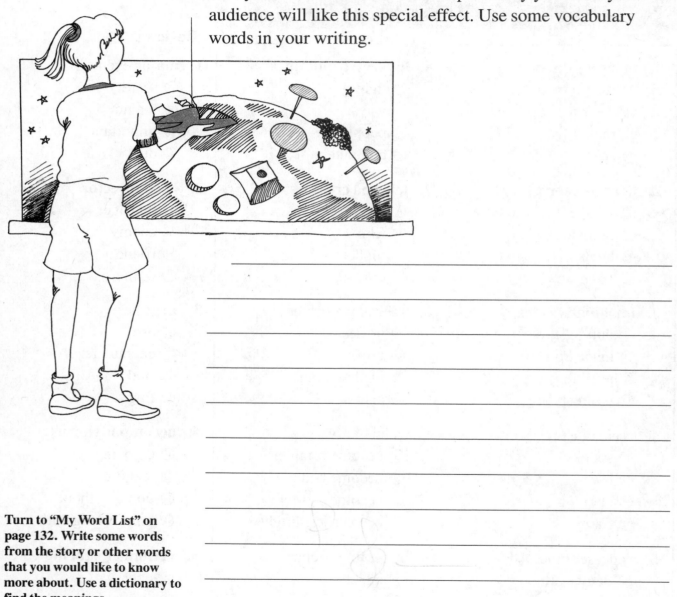

Turn to "My Word List" on page 132. Write some words from the story or other words that you would like to know more about. Use a dictionary to find the meanings.

★ Read the story below. Think about the meanings of the **boldfaced** words. ★

Tejano Music, a Hot Mix

Music is coming from the stage. A band is beginning to **rehearse**, or practice, a song. Is it rock and roll? Is it country music? Is it hip-hop? Is it jazz? The answer to all these questions is yes! The hot sound called Tejano is a mix of all of these kinds of music. It echoes in **auditoriums** where the music is performed in many cities and towns.

Tejano music represents a mix of cultures, too. You can hear a cheerful polka beat in some of the songs. Polka music came to Texas with the German people more than 100 years ago. Tejano music uses everything! The words in Tejano songs can be in Spanish or English. They can also be a mix of the two.

The word Tejano means "Texan." But it has come to mean more. One meaning is the special kind of music. Music lovers are loud in their praise of Tejano music. They have great interest in it. All this **enthusiasm** for the music is very strong near the border of the United States and Mexico. But the beat has become **internationally** known beyond these two countries. A Tejano group that has recorded an **album** of songs can quickly become famous. Their tape or compact disk of songs may be enjoyed by millions of people.

Tejano music has **appeal** for young and old alike. Adults like it. Many young people in their teens are fans. These **teenagers** may buy large pictures of their favorite singers. They look at these **posters** and dress like the Tejano stars.

The crowds at Tejano events never sit still. Chances are you will see **mobs** of people dancing when you hear the happy beat of Tejano. You will also hear long and loud clapping at the end of each song. This **applause** is for the singer, for the dancers, and for Tejano music.

★ Go back to the story. Underline the words or sentences that give you a clue to the meaning of each **boldfaced** word. ★

CONTEXT CLUES

Read each sentence. Look for clues to help you complete each sentence with a word from the box. Write the word on the line.

teenagers	enthusiasm	album	applause
posters	rehearse	mobs	internationally
appeal	auditoriums		

1. Many _teenagers_, often beginning at age thirteen, are big fans of Tejano music.

2. They show a lot of _enthusiasm_ for the hot, exciting mix of Tejano songs.

3. A Tejano group that records an _____ can be known all over the world.

4. Teens like to buy _____ that have the pictures of their favorite Tejano stars on them.

5. It is not unusual to read about _mobs_ of fans going to a Tejano concert.

6. Most concerts are held in _auditoriums_, large rooms with many seats and a stage.

7. Tejano musicians must _____ often so they can put on a good show.

8. Part of the _____ of Tejano music is that it is a mix of other kinds of music.

9. The Tejano sound has become _internationally_ known by people of all ages.

10. At a concert, it seems that the _applause_, or clapping, never seems to stop!

SYNONYMS AND ANTONYMS

Remember that **synonyms** are words that have the same or almost the same meaning. **Antonyms** are words that have opposite meanings. Each word below is paired with a **boldfaced** vocabulary word. If the two words are synonyms, put a check (√) under that heading. If the two words are antonyms, put a (√) under that heading.

	Synonyms	Antonyms
1. **applause** — clapping	_____	_____
2. **internationally** — locally	_____	_____
3. **enthusiasm** — energy	_____	_____
4. **teenagers** — adults	_____	_____
5. **posters** — pictures	_____	_____
6. **appeal** — disgust	_____	_____

WORD SUGGESTION

Some words have almost the same meaning, but one fits in a sentence better. Choose the word from each pair that best completes the sentence. Write it on the line.

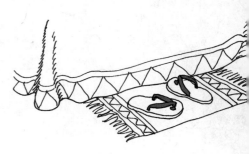

1. Fans filled with _____ for Tejano music live all over the world.   (interest, enthusiasm)

2. The musicians will want to _____ the music before the concert.   (rehearse, train)

3. There are three large _____ of my favorite singer covering the wall in my room.   (signs, posters)

4. There were _____ of people at the concert last night.   (mobs, herds)

ANALOGIES

Remember that an **analogy** shows how two words go together in the same way as two other words. Write the words from the box to complete the following analogies.

mobs	album	auditoriums	applause

1. Whistling is to mouth as _____ is to hands.
2. Swarms is to bugs as _____ is to people .
3. Book is to chapter as _____ is to song.
4. Theaters is to movies as _____ is to concerts.

DICTIONARY SKILLS

Remember that **guide words** are the two words at the top of each dictionary page. They show the first and last entries on that page. All the word entries in between are in alphabetical order. Look at the pairs of guide words. On the lines below each pair, write the words from the box that would appear on the same dictionary page. Be sure to put them in alphabetical order.

posters	internationally	applause	appeal
teenagers	auditoriums	album	mobs

active / gain   **hardy / useful**

1. _____   5. _____

2. _____   6. _____

3. _____   7. _____

4. _____   8. _____

Directions: Read each sentence carefully. Then choose the best answer to complete each sentence. Mark the space for the answer you have chosen.

 Tip Some tests have letters inside the answer circles. Fill in the circle next to your answer, covering the letter, too.

1. You **rehearse** before a _____.
   - Ⓐ concert
   - Ⓒ shoe
   - Ⓑ dream
   - Ⓓ cat

2. **Teenagers** are also _____.
   - Ⓕ plants
   - Ⓗ houses
   - Ⓖ students
   - Ⓙ schools

3. You may place **posters** on a _____.
   - Ⓐ jacket
   - Ⓒ wall
   - Ⓑ nest
   - Ⓓ dish

4. **Mobs** of Tejano fans can be _____.
   - Ⓕ melted
   - Ⓗ noisy
   - Ⓖ adopted
   - Ⓙ tasted

5. When an **album** is played, you can hear _____.
   - Ⓐ music
   - Ⓒ lights
   - Ⓑ nothing
   - Ⓓ chairs

6. One sign of **enthusiasm** is _____.
   - Ⓕ cheers
   - Ⓗ tears
   - Ⓖ yawns
   - Ⓙ anger

7. **Auditoriums** are used for _____.
   - Ⓐ accidents
   - Ⓒ cooking
   - Ⓑ parking
   - Ⓓ performances

8. The **appeal** of a concert is _____.
   - Ⓕ good food
   - Ⓗ sound sleep
   - Ⓖ live music
   - Ⓙ good sailing

9. If you are known **internationally**, you are known all over the _____.
   - Ⓐ school
   - Ⓒ sky
   - Ⓑ country
   - Ⓓ world

10. **Applause** is often _____.
    - Ⓕ sung
    - Ⓗ repaired
    - Ⓖ tight
    - Ⓙ loud

Review

1. Something that **flickers** _____.
   - Ⓐ bites
   - Ⓒ twinkles
   - Ⓑ sleeps
   - Ⓓ leaks

2. You can **assemble** a _____.
   - Ⓕ puzzle
   - Ⓗ raindrop
   - Ⓖ paper
   - Ⓙ breeze

Writing

Tejano music is one kind of music that people like to listen to. Some other kinds of music that people like are classical, rock, rap, and country and western. What kind of music do you like to listen to?

On the lines below, tell about your favorite kind of music. Tell why you like it, and what some of your favorite songs are. Use some vocabulary words in your writing.

Turn to "My Word List" on page 132. Write some words from the story or other words that you would like to know more about. Use a dictionary to find the meanings.

★ To review the words in Lessons 17–20, turn to page 129. ★

REVIEW

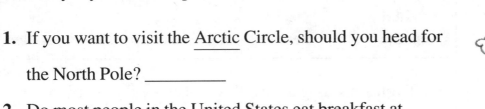

Read each question. Think about the meaning of the underlined word. Then use yes or no to answer the question. Use the Dictionary if you need help.

1. If you want to visit the Arctic Circle, should you head for the North Pole? _____

2. Do most people in the United States eat breakfast at twilight? _____

3. Is it a good idea to stand close to intense heat? _____

4. Can a human being jump rope indefinitely? _____

5. Would you be likely to find a lot of moisture in a desert? _____

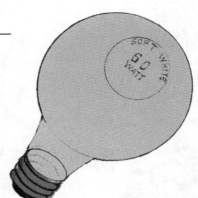

6. Would you find a display of light at a fireworks show? _____

7. If you want to make a doghouse cheaply, should you make it out of gold? _____

8. If you want to focus a beam of light, should you turn it off? _____

9. If a new haircut transforms your appearance, do you look different? _____

10. If your washing machine is broken, should you call a physician to repair it? _____

REVIEW

Read each clue. Then write the word from the box that fits the clue. Use the Dictionary if you need help.

gradual	healthy	gills	flee
appetite	ignore	nerves	scrape

1. If you are strong and well, you can use this word to describe yourself. _____

2. These parts of your body send messages to and from your brain. _____

3. If they lived only on land, tadpoles would not need these. _____

4. You might do this to a person who is boring. _____

5. If your stomach is growling and you feel hungry, you have this. _____

6. If you see lightning strike a tree beside you, you should do this. _____

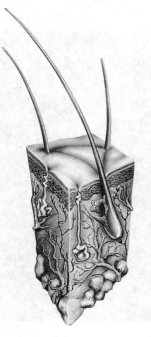

7. If you do this to your knee, the nurse might put a bandage on it. _____

8. This is the kind of change that happens over millions of years. _____

REVIEW

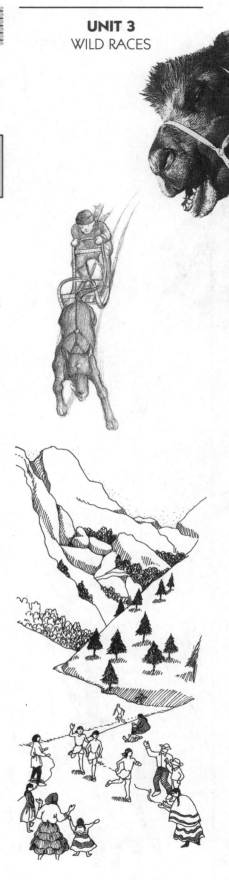

Read each clue. Then write the word from the box that fits the clue. Use the Dictionary if you need help.

triumphant	opponents	champion	gap
spectacle	orbited	rugged	shrieked

1. You might use this word to talk about a giant shooting star.

   _____

2. If you have ever screamed with excitement or fear, you did

   this. _____

3. If you want to walk on smooth ground, you should avoid

   this kind of path. _____

4. This is what the earth did to the sun in 365 days last year.

   _____

5. When you and a friend play each other in a game, you are

   these. _____

6. This is a name for the person who does not lose a contest.

   _____

7. This is probably how you would feel if you won an

   Olympic gold medal. _____

8. If you have this in your roof, you might get rained on.

   _____

REVIEW

Read each clue. Then write the word from the box that fits the clue. Use the Dictionary if you need help.

collapsed	crest	treacherous	caverns
avoid	gear	graze	evil

1. If you are standing at the top of a mountain, this is where you are. _____

2. You should probably not try to canoe on this kind of river.

   _____

3. Parents often tell their children to do this to a stranger.

   _____

4. You might use this word to describe a mean character in a fairy tale. _____

5. Horses, cattle, and sheep will do this if they have grass to eat. _____

6. When people go in these, they sometimes find bats.

   _____

7. If your ladder did this, you ended up on the ground.

   _____

8. If you are going on a camping trip, you need to take this.

   _____

Read each question. Think about the meaning of the underlined word. Then use yes or no to answer the question. Use the Dictionary if you need help.

1. Would you find an <u>opinion</u> in a vegetable garden? _____

2. If a company <u>advertised</u> a car, did they want people to buy it? _____

3. Would most people feel <u>pleasure</u> if they hit their finger with a hammer? _____

4. Would you expect an <u>honest</u> person to tell the truth? _____

5. If you wanted to create a video game, would an <u>imaginative</u> person come in handy? _____

6. To answer a test question correctly, should you give a <u>ridiculous</u> answer? _____

7. If you want to put a model airplane together, should you <u>assemble</u> it? _____

8. Would most people show <u>enthusiasm</u> for a meal of bread and water? _____

9. If a band wants to learn a new song, is it a good idea to <u>rehearse</u> it? _____

10. Would you expect to see <u>teenagers</u> riding tricycles? _____

REVIEW AND WRITE

You have read about many places in this book. Stories have taken you from the cold of the Arctic Circle to the warmth of the Hawaiian Islands. Which of these places would people like to visit?

On the lines below, write an advertisement for one of the places you have read about. Describe what this place looks like. Tell people why they should choose it as a place to visit. Use some of the vocabulary words you have learned.

_____

_____

_____

_____

_____

_____

_____

_____

_____

_____

_____

_____

_____

_____

_____

_____

MY WORD LIST

This is your word list. Here you can write words from the stories. You can also write other words that you would like to know more about. Use a dictionary to find the meaning of each word. Then write the meaning next to the word.

UNIT 1
BRIGHT LIGHTS

_____

_____

_____

_____

_____

_____

UNIT 2
CYCLES OF CHANGE

_____

_____

_____

_____

_____

MY WORD LIST

UNIT 3
WILD RACES

_____

_____

_____

_____

_____

_____

_____

UNIT 4
MOUNTAINS' MYSTERIES

_____

_____

_____

_____

_____

_____

_____

UNIT 5
ON STAGE

_____

_____

_____

_____

_____

_____

_____

DICTIONARY

ENTRY

Each word in a dictionary is called an **entry word**. Study the parts of an entry in the sample shown below. Think about how each part will help you when you read and write.

① **Entry Word** An entry word is boldfaced. A dot is used to divide the word into syllables.

② **Pronunciation** This special spelling shows you how to say the word. Look at the pronunciation key below. It tells you the symbols that stand for sounds.

③ **Part of Speech** The abbreviation tells you the part of speech. In this entry *v.* stands for verb.

④ **Words with Spelling Changes** When the spelling of a word changes after *-ed* or *-ing* is added, the spelling is shown in an entry.

⑤ **Definition** A definition is given for each entry word. The definition tells what the word means.

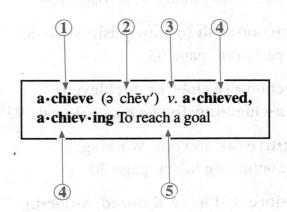

PRONUNCIATION KEY

A **pronunciation key** is a helpful tool. It shows you the symbols, or special signs, for the sounds in English. Next to each symbol is a sample word for that sound. Use the key to help you with the pronunciation given after each entry word.

a	at, bad	d	dear, soda, bad
ā	ape, pain, day, break	f	five, defend, leaf, off, cough, elephant
ä	father, car, heart	g	game, ago, fog, egg
âr	care, pair, bear, their, where	h	hat, ahead
e	end, pet, said, heaven, friend	hw	white, whether, which
ē	equal, me, feet, team, piece, key	j	joke, enjoy, gem, page, edge
i	it, big, English, hymn	k	kite, bakery, seek, tack, cat
ī	ice, fine, lie, my	l	lid, sailor, feel, ball, allow
îr	ear, deer, here, pierce	m	man, family, dream
o	odd, hot, watch	n	not, final, pan, knife
ō	old, oat, toe, low	ng	long, singer, pink
ô	coffee, all, taught, law, fought	p	pail, repair, soap, happy
ôr	order, fork, horse, story, pour	r	ride, parent, wear, more, marry
oi	oil, toy	s	sit, aside, pets, cent, pass
ou	out, now	sh	shoe, washer, fish, mission, nation
u	up, mud, love, double	t	tag, pretend, fat, button, dressed
ū	use, mule, cue, feud, few	th	thin, panther, both
ü	rule, true, food	<u>th</u>	this, mother, smooth
u̇	put, wood, should	v	very, favor, wave
ûr	burn, hurry, term, bird, word, courage	w	wet, weather, reward
ə	about, taken, pencil, lemon, circus	y	yes, onion
b	bat, above, job	z	zoo, lazy, jazz, rose, dogs, houses
ch	chin, such, match	zh	vision, treasure, seizure

133

DICTIONARY

A

ac•com•pa•ny•ing (ə kum´pə nē ing) *adj.* Going along with. page 108

ac•com•plish (ə kom´plish) *v.* To do; carry out. page 95

a•chieve (ə chēv´) *v.* **a•chieved, a•chiev•ing** To reach a goal. page 95

ac•tive (ak´tiv) *adj.* Working; continuing to act. page 30

a•dore (ə dôr´) *v.* **a•dored, a•dor•ing** To love very much. page 36

ad•ver•tise (ad´vər tīz´) *v.* **ad•ver•tised, ad•ver•tis•ing** To sell a product by sending a message through television, radio, or newspapers. page 102

a•gree•ment (ə grē´mənt) *n.* An understanding between two or more people. page 108

al•bum (al´bəm) *n.* A collection of recorded songs. page 119

al•gae (al´jē) *n.* Small water plants. page 42

ap•peal (ə pēl´) *n.* Charm; attractiveness. page 119

ap•pe•tite (ap´i tīt´) *n.* The wish for food; hunger. page 37

ap•plause (ə plôz´) *n.* Clapping to show approval. page 119

arch (ärch) *n.* A curved shape. page 18

Arc•tic (ärk´tik, är´tik) *n.* The area around the North Pole. page 6

ar•riv•al (ə rī´vəl) *n.* The time of coming to a place; the end of a journey. page 78

ar•tis•tic (är tis´tik) *adj.* Done with good design and skill. page 23

as•cend (ə send´) *v.* To climb. page 78

as•sem•ble (ə sem´bəl) *v.* **as•sem•bled, as•sem•bling** To put together. page 114

a•stride (ə strīd´) *prep.* Sitting with one leg on each side of. page 85

as•tro•naut (as´trə nôt´) *n.* A person who travels on a spacecraft. page 66

at•tempt (ə tempt´) *v.* To try. page 60

au•di•to•ri•um (ô´di tôr´ē əm) *n.* A large room where people watch plays and concerts. page 119

a•void (ə void´) *v.* To keep away from. page 95

B

be•gin•ner (bi gin´ər) *n.* A person who does something for the first time. page 95

bi•ol•o•gist (bī o;st) *n.* A person who studies animal life. page 42

blot (blot) *v.* **blot·ted, blot·ting.** To hide; cover up. page 84

breath·tak·ing (breth´tā´king) *adj.* Wonderful; splendid. page 78

bright·ness (brīt´nis) *n.* The amount of light. page 6

broad·cast (brôd´kast´) *n.* A program sent out by a television station. page 102

C

cam·el (kam´əl) *n.* A large desert animal that has one or two humps on its back. page 54

car·bon (kär´bən) *n.* A very common element. Pencil leads and coal are mostly carbon. page 13

cav·ern (kav´ərn) *n.* A large cave. page 90

cham·pi·on (cham´pē ən) *n.* The winner of a contest; the person who comes in first. page 54

chan·nel (chan´əl) *n.* The special set of electrical waves used to send out programs from a television station. page 102

cheap·ly (chēp´lē) *adv.* In a way that costs little. page 12

coax (kōks) *v.* To urge; speak softly to persuade. page 54

col·lapse (kə laps´) *v.* **col·lapsed, col·laps·ing** To fall in. page 90

com·mu·ni·ca·tion (kə mū´ni kā´shən) *n.* Information that is sent and received. page 102

com·pe·ti·tion (kom´pi tish´ən) *n.* Contest; race. page 54

con·cen·trate (kon´sən trāt´) *v.* **con·cen·trat·ed, con·cen·trat·ing** To pay close attention to; work carefully. page 95

con·quer (kong´kər) *v.* To win; to gain control of. page 66

cre·a·tor (krē ā´tər) *n.* A person who makes something that has not been made before. page 114

crest (krest) *n.* The top part of a mountain. page 78

crust (krust) *n.* The top layer of the earth. page 90

cur·rent (kûr´ənt, kur´ənt) *n.* The movement of electricity through a wire. page 12

D

dai·ly (dā´lē) *adj.* Happening every day. page 6

dart (därt) *v.* To move quickly and suddenly. page 42

da·ta (dā´tə, dat´ə) *n.* Facts; information. page 66

de•lay (di lā´) *n.* A wait until a later time. page 66

de•pos•it (di poz´it) *v.* To put something down. page 90

de•serve (di zûrv´) *v.* **de•served, de•serv•ing** To have a right to. page 95

de•sire (di zīr´) *n.* A strong wish; longing. page 95

des•per•ate•ly (des´pər it lē, des´prit lē) *adv.* In a fearful, reckless way. page 85

de•ter•mi•na•tion (di tûr´mə nā´shən) *n.* Great willpower in doing something. page 71

de•vel•op•ment (di vel´əp mənt) *n.* The process of growing up. page 42

di•rec•tor (di rek´tər, dī rek´tər) *n.* The person who controls and directs others' work. page 109

disc jock•ey (disk jok´ē) *n.* A radio announcer who plays music. page 108

dis•mount (dis mount´) *v.* To get down or off. page 54

dis•play (di splā´) *n.* A show. page 18

dis•solve (di zolv´) *v.* **dis•solved, dis•solv•ing** To turn into a liquid; melt. page 114

E

ed•u•ca•tion•al (ej´ə kā´shə nəl) *adj.* Having to do with learning; giving knowledge. page 102

ee•rie (îr´ē) *adj.* Strange; scary. page 114

en•dure (en dùr´) *v.* **en•dured, en•dur•ing** To put up with. page 71

en•thu•si•asm (en thü´zē az´əm) *n.* Great interest and energy. page 119

en•try (en´trē) *n.* **en•tries** A person who takes part in a contest. page 54

en•vi•ron•ment (en vī´rən mənt, en vī´ərn mənt) *n.* The place where something lives; surroundings. page 42

e•rupt (i rupt´) *v.* To throw out melted rock. page 30

e•vil (ē´vəl) *adj.* Bad; wicked. page 84

ex•tend (ek stend´) *v.* To stretch in a direction. page 90

F

fade (fād) *v.* **fad•ed, fad•ing** To become less bright. page 114

flee (flē) *v.* **fled, flee•ing** To run away. page 30

flick•er (flik´ər) *v.* To grow bright and dim in an unsteady way. page 114

fo•cus (fō′kəs) *v.* To aim a light beam in a particular direction. page 23

func•tion (fungk′shən) *n.* Job; usual work. page 47

fur•nace (fûr′nis) *n.* A box that holds a very hot fire. page 30

fur•nish (fûr′nish) *v.* To give. page 12

G

gain (gān) *v.* To catch up; come closer. page 61

gap (gap) *n.* The space between two things. page 60

gear (gîr) *n.* Equipment. page 95

gen•er•a•tion (jen′ə rā′shən) *n.* All the people born about the same time. page 102

ge•ol•o•gist (jē ol′ə jist) *n.* A person who studies the structure of the earth. page 90

gill (gil) *n.* The part of a tadpole or fish that lets it breathe underwater. page 42

gland (gland) *n.* A part of the body that takes out materials from the blood for another use in the body. page 47

glimpse (glimps) *n.* A short, quick look; a glance. page 61

goal (gōl) *n.* Something wished for; aim. page 71

gorge (gôrj) *n.* A deep, narrow opening between two mountains; a steep valley. page 90

grad•u•al (graj′ü əl) *adj.* Happening slowly. page 42

graze (grāz) *v.* **grazed, graz•ing** To eat grass for food. page 84

growth (grōth) *n.* Process of becoming larger as time passes. page 42

H

har•dy (här′dē) *adj.* **har•di•er, har•di•est** Tough; able to put up with hard conditions. page 71

haunt•ing (hôn′ting) *adj.* Strange and hard to forget. page 85

health•y (hel′thē) *adj.* **health•i•er, health•i•est** Well; free from sickness. page 47

heave (hēv) *v.* **heaved, heav•ing** To push. page 90

he•ro•ic (hi rō′ik) *adj.* Very great; far beyond the ordinary. page 78

home•town (hōm′toun′) *n.* The town in which a person was born. page 37

hon•est (on′ist) *adj.* Truthful; fair. page 108

ho•ri•zon (hə rī′zən) *n.* The place where earth and sky meet. page 6

horse•shoe (hôrs´shü´) *n.* A U-shaped metal plate that is nailed to horses' feet. page 13

I

ig•nore (ig nôr´) *v.* **ig•nored, ig•nor•ing** To pay no attention to. page 36

i•mag•i•na•tive (i maj´ə nə tiv) *adj.* Able to think of new things easily. page 114

im•press (im pres´) *v.* To have a strong effect on the feelings; amaze. page 23

in•cred•i•ble (in kred´ə bəl) *adj.* Hard to believe. page 78

in•def•i•nite•ly (in def´ə nit lē) *adv.* Without any end or limit. page 13

in•hab•it (in hab´it) *v.* To live in or on. page 42

in•spi•ra•tion (in´spə rā´shən) *n.* A person who is looked up to and who makes others want to do difficult things. page 95

in•su•late (in´sə lāt´) *v.* **in•su•lat•ed, in•su•lat•ing** To keep from becoming too hot or too cold. page 47

in•tense (in tens´) *adj.* Very strong; very great. page 12

in•ter•na•tion•al•ly (in´tər nash´ə nəl ē) *adv.* Between or among nations. page 119

in•ven•tor (in ven´tər) *n.* A person who thinks up new devices or machines. page 13

in•vis•i•ble (in viz´ə bəl) *adj.* Not able to be seen. page 47

is•sue (ish´ü) *v.* **is•sued, is•su•ing** To send or give out. page 85

L

la•goon (lə gün´) *n.* A small, quiet body of water connected to a larger body of water. page 42

launch (lônch) *v.* To send into space. page 66

la•va (lä´və, lav´ə) *n.* The melted rock that flows from a volcano. page 30

life•time (līf´tīm´) *n.* The time a person is alive. page 47

lo•ca•tion (lō kā´shən) *n.* Place where something is. page 6

loch (lok) *n. Scottish* A lake. page 85

lone•li•ness (lōn´lē nis) *n.* Being alone and wanting to be with others. page 71

lunge (lunj) *v.* **lunged, lung•ing** To move forward suddenly. page 54

M

ma•jor (mā´jər) *adj.* Larger; more important. page 108

man•go (mang´gō) *n.* **man•goes** or **man•gos** The fruit of a tree that grows in the tropics. page 36

mar•vel (mär´vəl) *v.* To be filled with wonder; be amazed. page 23

ma•ture (mə chùr´, me tyùr´, mə tùr´) *adj.* Grown-up; full-grown. page 47

mob (mob) *n.* A large crowd. page 119

mois•ture (mois´chər) *n.* Wetness; dampness. page 18

mol•ten (mōl´tən) *adj.* Melted; turned into a liquid by heat. page 30

moon•lit (mün´lit´) *adj.* Lighted by the moon. page 6

moun•tain•top (mount´ən top´) *n.* The top of a mountain. page 78

mulch (mulch) *n.* Leaves or straw put around the bottom of a tree to protect it and help it grow. page 36

N

na•tion (nā´shən) *n.* Country; people having the same government. page 66

nerve (nûrv) *n.* A body part that carries signals between the brain and spine to parts like the eyes and muscles. page 47

net•work (net´wûrk´) *n.* Television stations that work together to send out the same program. page 102

night•fall (nīt´fôl´) *n.* Dusk; the time when night comes. page 6

nor•mal (nôr´məl) *adj.* Usual; expected. page 47

O

ob•serve (əb zûrv´) *v.* **ob•served, ob•serv•ing** To see; notice. page 18

op•er•a•tor (op´ə rā´tər) *n.* The person who controls a machine. page 23

o•pin•ion (ə pin´yən) *n.* What a person thinks or believes. page 108

op•po•nent (ə pō´nənt) *n.* A person you are competing against in a contest. page 71

or•bit (ôr´bit) *v.* To travel around in a circle. page 66

or•i•gin (ôr´i jin, or´i jin) *n.* Beginning; starting point. page 90

out•run (out´run´) *v.* **out•ran, out•run, out•run•ning** To run faster than. page 54

o•ver•come (ō´vər kum´) *v.* **o•ver•came, o•ver•com•ing** To get the better of; win over. page 71

o•ver•flow (ō´vər flō´) *v.* To fill up and run over. page 30

ox•y•gen mask (ok´sə jən mask) *n.* A device that gives air to mountain climbers, pilots, and others at high altitudes. page 78

139

P

per•mit (pər mit´) *v.* **per•mit•ted, per•mit•ting** To let; allow. page 60

phys•i•cal (fiz´i kəl) *adj.* Having to do with the body. page 95

phy•si•cian (fə zish´ən). *n.* A doctor of medicine. page 23

plat•i•num (plat´ə nəm) *n.* A heavy silver-white precious metal. page 12

pleas•ure (plezh´ər) *n.* Enjoyment; the feeling of being pleased. page 102

post•er (pōs´tər) *n.* A large printed piece of paper that can be put up on a wall. page 119

proc•ess (pros´es, prō´ses) *n.* A group of actions done in a certain order. page 114

pro•duce (prə düs´, prə dūs´) *v.* To make; to give forth. page 23

Q

qual•i•fy (kwol´ə fī´) *v.* **qual•i•fied, qual•i•fy•ing** To show that you are fit for something. page 54

R

rac•er (rā´sər) *n.* A person who takes part in a contest of speed. page 60

rain•drop (rān´drop´) *n.* A drop of rain. page 18

rain•storm (rān´stôrm´) *n.* A storm that has much rain. page 18

re•al•is•tic (rē´ə lis´tik) *adj.* Looking like real people or things; lifelike. page 23

re•cov•er (ri kuv´ər) *v.* To get well. page 37

re•flect (ri flekt´) *v.* To send back. page 18

ref•uge (ref´ūj) *n.* A place that is safe from danger. page 30

re•gain (rē gān´) *v.* To get back. page 61

re•hearse (ri hûrs´) *v.* **re•hearsed, re•hears•ing** To practice over and over. page 119

rep•re•sent (rep´ri zent´) *v.* To stand for; act in place of. page 114

re•view (ri vū´) *v.* To look at carefully. page 108

ri•dic•u•lous (ri dik´yə ləs) *adj.* Too silly to believe; laughable. page 102

risk (risk) *n.* The chance of danger or harm. page 60

ro•bust (rō bust´, rō´bust) *adj.* Healthy and strong. page 37

rug•ged (rug´id) *adj.* Rough; uneven. page 71

S

sat•el•lite (sat´ə līt´) *n.* An object made by people that is sent into space by rocket. page 66

scrape (skrāp) *v.* **scraped, scrap•ing** To scratch; rub in a rough way. page 47

short•cut (shôrt´kut´) *n.* A way that is quicker or shorter. page 60

shriek (shrēk) *v.* To scream; make a loud, shrill sound. page 61

sit•u•a•tion (sich´ü ā´shən) *n.* Circumstance; problem that needs to be handled. page 102

slope (slōp) *n.* The side of a mountain. page 30

smoth•er (smuth´ər) *v.* To cover completely. page 84

soul (sōl) *n.* Life energy; where a person's feelings and thoughts begin. page 37

space•craft (spās´kraft´) *n.* Rocket; a machine that travels in space. page 66

spec•ta•cle (spek´tə kəl) *n.* Something to look at; an amazing sight. page 54

spec•tac•u•lar (spek tak´yə lər) *adj.* Wonderful to see. page 18

spell•bound (spel´bound´) *adj.* So interested that one cannot speak or move. page 23

stal•lion (stal´yən) *n.* A male horse. page 85

sun•rise (sun´rīz´) *n.* The appearance of the sun in the morning; the beginning of day. page 6

sun•set (sun´set´) *n.* The disappearance of the sun in the evening; the beginning of night. page 6

T

tech•nique (tek nēk´) *n.* A way to do something; method. page 114

teen•ag•er (tēn´ā´jər) *n.* A person from 13 through 19 years old. page 119

theme (thēm) *n.* A melody that identifies a show or musical group. page 109

trans•form (trans fôrm´) *v.* To change greatly. page 23

treach•er•ous (trech´ər əs) *adj.* Dangerous. page 78

tri•um•phant (trī um´fənt) *adj.* Successful. page 66

twi•light (twī´līt´) *n.* The time between sunset and complete darkness. page 6

U

up•hill (up´hil´) *adv.* Up the side of a mountain or hill. page 78

up•ward (up´wərd) *adv.* Toward a higher place. page 90

urge (ûrj) *v.* **urged**, **urg•ing** To ask or tell strongly. page 108

V

vic•to•ry (vik´tə rē) *n.* **vic•to•ries** A win; success. page 71

vis•i•ble (viz´ə bəl) *adj.* Able to be seen. page 18

viv•id (viv´id) *adj.* Bright; brilliant. page 18

W

warn•ing (wôr´ning) *n.* Sign of possible danger. page 30

wea•ri•ness (wîr´ē nis) *n.* Tiredness; worn out feeling. page 71

wel•fare (wel´fâr´) *n.* Health and happiness. page 37

wiz•ard (wiz´ərd) *n.* A person who can do magic. page 13